THE PATTERDALE TERRIER

THE
PATTERDALE
TERRIER

Seán Frain

SWAN·HILL
PRESS

First published in the UK in 2004
by Swan Hill Press, an imprint of Quiller Publishing Ltd

Reprinted 2005

British Library Cataloguing-in-Publication Data

A catalogue record for this book
is available from the British Library

ISBN 1 904057 57 8

Photographs: The majority of these have been supplied by
the author, but thanks must go to Max Buck, Brian Nuttall
and Gary Middleton, also Barry Wild, for additional
photographs.

Typeset by Phoenix Typesetting, Auldgirth, Dumfriesshire
Printed in England by St Edmundsbury Press Ltd,
Bury St Edmunds, Suffolk

Swan Hill Press

An imprint of Quiller Publishing Ltd.
Wykey House, Wykey, Shrewsbury, SY4 1JA
Tel: 01939 261616 Fax: 01939 261606
E-mail: info@quillerbooks.com
Website: www.swanhillbooks.com

Dedicated to the memory of Frank Buck and Cyril Breay;
for leaving us a race of truly game terriers.

ACKNOWLEDGEMENTS

Many thanks to Max Buck, Gary Middleton, Brian Nuttall, Barry Wild, Roger Westmoreland, and Danny Sykes for their valuable contributions to the material in this book. Also, thanks are due to Ruth Middleton and Wendy Buck for their generous hospitality. Grateful thanks to John Hill who guided me through the maze that is the internet, and to the editorial staff of *The Countryman's Weekly* for their contribution regarding photographs and material which has already appeared in that publication. Also, I am indebted to Clare Sawers for providing me with a few photos and for putting a word in with 'the gaffer'!

CONTENTS

	Acknowledgements	vi
	Introduction	ix
1	Fellhunting Country	1
2	The Original Patterdale	22
3	Origins of Modern Patterdales	61
4	The Modern Patterdale	81
5	Patterdales and Other Breeds	120
6	The Versatile Patterdale	128
7	Patterdales and Shows	153
8	Patterdales and the Family	163
9	Patterdales in America	171
10	The Puppy and its Training	177
11	Breeding	194
12	Common Ailments and Injuries	206
	Appendices	
	1 Bibliography	210
	2 Useful Addresses	210
	3 Breeding of Nuttall's Patterdales	211
	Index	212

Gary Middleton with a black and tan bitch; a near replica to Wilkinson's Nettle, the original type known as Patterdale terriers.

INTRODUCTION

Dave Harcombe, in his book, *The World of The Working Terrier*, states that, regarding the red and black slape and hard-coated terriers bred down from the dogs of Frank Buck and Cyril Breay, the name 'Patterdale terrier' is now here to stay, and I can only agree with him. These terriers are so widely known by this name that it is pointless anymore to ramble on (though I will undoubtedly do so, for this issue still rouses passion in many fell terrier enthusiasts) about the rights and wrongs of such labelling. These earth dogs, despite the fact that they have only a slight connection with the tiny village of Patterdale in Cumbria, were given this name many years ago and it has stuck, much to the annoyance of many of the older generation of fell hunters who were breeding and working fell types of terrier long before Cyril Breay made his show debut with his dogs.

Gary Middleton was at the show in Patterdale when Breay first exhibited this new type of terrier in this district. He was standing with Anthony Barker and Sid Wilkinson and the pair of them turned to him and asked (not in a derogatory sense) what on earth was that that Cyril had with him. When asked about his dog, Cyril Breay remarked that it was simply a type of fell terrier and never referred to it as a Patterdale. In fact, the late Anthony Barker farmed just outside this village and he would surely have recognised a Patterdale terrier, as would Sid Wilkinson who lived just up the road at Glenridding.

This terrier was Bingo, a deep, chestnut red terrier who was one of the gamest workers the Buck and Breay strain ever produced; a dog bred by Frank Buck and given to Breay who worked him enthusiastically with the Lunesdale hunt, which are kennelled just up the road from Sedbergh. Buck called him Bing and this is how he was commonly known, though Cyril Breay changed his name to Bingo after Frank gave the dog to him. Bingo killed many foxes before he perished in a tussle with a fox in the Lunesdale country. No doubt the many previous encounters with foxes had weakened Bing's jaw somewhat, for it finally gave during this titanic struggle and he was dead when Roger Westmoreland finally reached him.

Middleton states that Bingo was a very 'typey' terrier and of a very attractive deep red colour. This colour continues to crop up on some of the descendants of Bingo who mated several bitches before he died and who played a major part in the creation of the modern strains of what are now known as Patterdales. Like it or not, as Harcombe says, this name is here to stay.

The truth is, Patterdale terriers sprang up from the original fell strains and they retain, even to this day, many of the qualities of the old Cumbrian hunt terriers which have played such an important part in helping to keep down the hardy fox population of this area. The old fell strains were the gamest in the world and this is reflected in the modern Patterdale terrier which has grown in popularity at an incredible rate during recent years, now being extensively used throughout the country. However, it was in the North of England that the strains originated and their birthplace is an incredibly difficult country to hunt, testing both the constitution, and the gameness, of any terrier required to work such an area successfully.

1

FELLHUNTING COUNTRY

Mountain range after mountain range, rivers and becks flowing from the heartlands and filling after the heavy rain that falls without much warning in this part of the world the large number of lakes, some huge, others small, that are found throughout Cumbria, with a massive number of tiny tarns dotted around, all of which give this region its other, possibly more familiar, name the English Lake District.

Craggy peaks rise sharply into a frequently stormy sky, very often mist covered, for days on end, and giving them an eerie, even hostile appearance which frightened off many of the early tourists who stumbled upon this area and who wrote of its fearsome, unwelcoming landscape. Huge mounds of scree litter the fell sides and make it almost impossible for the fellwalker, or, indeed, the follower of a fellpack, to cross the steep valleys. Some of the worst scree-beds I have ever come across in the Lakes are found deep in the heart of the incredibly beautiful Borrowdale valley where high mountain peaks stretch into the distance.

I crossed these scree-beds extremely carefully, alongside my fell terriers, and, consequently, made slow progress as I followed, or attempted to follow, the Blencathra foxhounds who were busy searching the crags high above for the presence of a skulking fox. Foxes often spend the day sleeping amongst these crags, or sometimes they will seek sanctuary at such places when hard pressed by hounds. Hounds will sometimes succeed in shifting their quarry from these difficult spots, though on many occasions Reynard has to be given best. Now and again though, especially if a terrier has a gift for climbing a crag, this will be allowed to seek out its foe and bolt it from its hiding place. Many good terriers have perished when working out foxes from such dangerous locations, and so there are many crags that are no longer deemed safe enough to allow terrier, or, indeed, hound, access, no matter how many foxes are seeking safety there.

Terriers must be agile if they are to work rockpiles and borrans successfully.

Now and again a terrier, or, more likely a hound and possibly a few hounds, will follow a fox out onto a crag and they will then be unable to make their way back to safer ground. In the old days, ropes were used to lower one of the more stout-hearted followers who would then rescue these trapped hounds. Nowadays though, a helicopter is required to lift off trapped hounds and only a few years ago some of the Ullswater pack had to be airlifted from Black Crag, a forbidding place above Patterdale, after they had followed a fox onto the narrow rock ledges. Honister Crag, above the Honister pass in the Melbreak country, is another fearsome spot which has claimed the lives of hounds and terriers over the years. Sometimes hounds, close to their quarry and giving everything they have in order to catch up with it, will be unable to stop themselves when a fox drops down onto a crag, sometimes falling hundreds of feet to instant death. This is quite a rare occurrence however, for hounds know their country better than their huntsman.

One wrong move on these scree-beds can easily result in a broken ankle and then you are in trouble. It was hard going and a little unnerving, crossing these vast mounds of scree, especially when I could feel them giving and moving under my feet. You can imagine how amazed I was when a little later the hounds returned and crossed those self-same scree-beds without flinching, running across them almost unhindered in their search for that elusive fox, which had earlier passed under the crags above and had quickly gone out over the felltop towards Newlands, where it eventually found safe sanctuary inside a big, rough bield. There are many very bad places in this area which are just too dangerous for a terrier to be put in, so the Huntsman was forced to whip them off and try for another.

I suppose it is the centuries of breeding hounds for hunting on the fells that has produced abilities of this kind, for these hounds are as native as Cumbrian slate and they instinctively know the ground on which they hunt, and thus are well adapted to crossing it. Those scree-beds are huge, not just in height, but also in the area of ground they cover and the crags immense and popular with rock climbers. Many succeed, while others suffer defeat, even injury and occasionally death.

Rocks jut out of the ground almost everywhere one looks, their jagged edges rising menacingly yet those hounds have the task of not only finding foxes in such places: narrow ledges sometimes a hundred feet or more off the ground, deep ghylls, dangerously steep and often slippery, but they also must follow the roused fox and even catch him, even though he is very fleet-of-foot and incredibly cunning too. These tough hill foxes have been born to these conditions over centuries, and so are well suited to such a landscape. Hounds succeed and catch many foxes, though it is true to say that many also escape. Some, however, are either found, or are driven, to ground and this is when the hardy fell terrier comes into its own. The ancestors of the Patterdale terrier would be required to find their fox inside some of these extremely deep and vast earths and bolt, or kill their fox, should it stand its ground far below the feet of the hunters who were now helpless to do anything more to catch their quarry. A terrier in this situation is all alone and must do its best to succeed. Some of the gamer terriers will quickly kill a fox which refuses to bolt, while others will bay and tease their quarry in the hopes that the diggers will reach it before long. Many Lakeland earths, even the borrans, are diggable, but most are not. A terrier must deal with its fox and

John Parker (J.P.) heading for the fells above the beautiful Borrowdale valley. (Blencathra foxhounds).

get out as best it can, or be there until death brings release. It is an incredibly difficult country for hounds and Huntsmen to work, but much more so for the game terrier which has its quarry to ground in such a landscape!

While out with the Blencathra one cold February day, I got talking to an old gentleman who had followed this hunt for as long as he could remember. He was one of the Porter family of Borrowdale and even now, into his eighties, he was still able to climb out onto the high felltops and watch the hounds and their Huntsman at work. He told me of the first occasion when he had watched hounds hunt the local fells and his eyes suddenly lit up as he reminisced of those long past days which, in so many ways, were better times.

Jim Dalton was still Huntsman then and, as he came down the Borrowdale valley with his pack, which were following the scent of the hunted fox with great eagerness indeed, the local teacher had allowed the class to go out into the fresh winter air and watch the pack at work. He was fascinated with what he saw and this memory had stuck in his mind and was as clear as the day on which it had occurred, all these years later. He can remember the silver-haired Huntsman, at this time getting towards the end of an illustrious career, soon arriving at a borran by the side of a steep ghyll which was being marked by hounds, the zealous terriers coupled at his side and all hoping they were going to get a turn to ground.

Sure enough, a terrier was loosed from its couples and shortly afterwards it disappeared into the borran, quickly finding its fox and getting stuck into it eagerly. Although they were quite a way from this earth, a borran I could clearly see on the hillside opposite from where we stood, high up above the crags on Chapel fell, he recalled being able to hear the terrier at work as it bayed in order to bolt its quarry. However, this fox had gained quite a stronghold and was not going to shift easily, and so

A Patterdale terrier disappearing below ground in search of its fox.

digging operations commenced, the school kids now being taken back to class in order to carry on with their education.

As is a common occurrence up in the fells, the borran proved to be difficult to effect a way into and so operations continued well into the night. He could remember the oil lanterns placed all around the borran and lighting up their way, high on that fell-side. He couldn't recall if they eventually got their fox or not, but all he knew was that that dig lasted for several hours, long after darkness had set in, and that Dalton's terriers were some of the gamest in the fells at that time, so it seems reasonable to assume that they eventually broke through to the terrier and its quarry, finally securing the brush of that predator of the fells. To succeed in digging out foxes from such vast, near-impossible places, is an incredible feat, yet many many digs successfully occur in such circumstances every season in the fells. Lakeland is truly a place of hardy hillmen who breed and work even hardier hounds and terriers, continuing the never-ending fight to protect the livestock of these hill shepherds and farmers.

At the same time, many foxes have to be left and given best, allowing them to run for another day, though any fell Huntsman does not like doing so, for it is his job to reduce the fox population as much as possible, in readiness for lambing time which usually begins in late March. Not that foxes are to be exterminated. Anyone who wishes to exterminate a species has no place hunting a fellpack, for the true fell Huntsman is a countryman at heart and has a deep respect for the quarry he hunts. Being a true countryman, however, he also realises what serious problems foxes can cause when they prey on farm livestock, and so he is happy to provide a service to the shepherds and farmers of his hunt country, in order to keep that predation to a minimum.

Amongst the rocks, thick vegetation grows in abundance, though there is little on the higher slopes to interest the shepherd who has sheep to fatten in readiness for the sales. Sheep do feed on the higher slopes though, but usually it is the hardy Herdwick or the Swaledale that is kept in this region. These survive well enough, but very often the shepherd must send his flock to richer pastures in the low country where they can be fattened up, which cuts down quite a bit on any profits made when it comes to selling, for fattening grazing rights do not come cheap.

Bracken, dense and sometimes chest height, is found all over the landscape of the Lake District and, especially during early autumn, can make the going quite difficult for the foot follower who is intent on keeping close to hounds. Foxes can give hounds the run-around all day in this stuff and for this reason they will usually hunt higher ground until the bracken has died off somewhat as autumn progresses. The Coniston foxhounds have quite a bit of low country towards the lower end of Windermere, around the Cartmel fell area, which is best left until later in the autumn when the bracken has begun to die back, for this plant grows prolifically in such places.

Dense gorse is another problem in some areas for those attempting to keep in touch with the pack. A problem it may be to the fellpack follower, but nevertheless we would not be without it, for gorse is extremely good cover for holding foxes and is very often a 'sure find'. When out with the Coniston pack around the Cartmel fell area, hounds flew into a dense gorse covert on a steep hillside and quickly found, pushing their fox out right in front of the Huntsman and a few hounds he had with him. I was standing just behind and got a quick glimpse of Reynard as he turned on his brush and disappeared again, finally leaving covert and taking hounds on a very long hunt which took them all the way to the shores of Windermere, before heading back into the forest above. This fox eventually eluded capture, but it was a cracking find and a superb hunt, though the fast action was difficult to keep up with.

The Langdales, a very rocky and mountainous wilderness full of extremely high crags and loose mounds of scree, is a place where gorse grows in abundance and you can be fairly sure of more than one fox using these coverts in order to rest after a long night on the prowl.

Deep heather, especially growing around craggy areas, is found in profusion in places and is particularly dense in some parts of the low country where it competes with gorse, bracken and forestry, with some scattered woodland. Foxes flourish in these areas and I once watched as hounds hunted several around a small wood which was overgrown with bracken and deep heather, hunting them for a very long time, for they were unable to push them out into the open. In the end the Huntsman was forced to call hounds out and moved on to try for another. Again, this was in the low country where dense undergrowth makes fox control a difficult task. So difficult, in fact, that, in order to keep on top of the fox population, fox drives are organised in this part of the Lakes on a fairly regular basis through the winter months, for hounds have large areas to cover and they can only spend so

Chris, the trainee underkeeper, with Fell and the fox he bolted. Bolting foxes with terriers and shooting them is a very effective way of controlling their numbers.

much time at one place. This is not a recent measure, however, for fox shoots have taken place in the Lake District for decades.

When Anthony Barker was Huntsman of the Ullswater foxhounds during the Second World War, he was sometimes called upon to drive foxes to guns with his hounds, as were other Huntsmen, for foxes increased considerably during the war years because they were hunted far less than previously, as many of the hunt servants and terriermen were on the front line. At times, especially when woodland or forestry was drawn by hounds, as many as a dozen foxes would be shot, while hounds would also account for one or two. Huntsmen like Anthony Barker were not keen on this task, though, for they were constantly worried about their hounds, or even themselves, getting shot. Nevertheless, they continued to carry out this vital role in controlling foxes and large numbers were taken using this, one of the most effective of methods.

At the moment there is much controversy surrounding the shooting of foxes, the worry being that many can be injured and thus go on to die long, lingering deaths. With hounds, however, this risk is reduced to practically nil, for an injured fox can be hunted to where it has earth'd, or laid up in covert, and can be finished off quickly, thus ending its suffering. Gunpacks play a vital role in humane fox control, but the fellpacks were using this method long before gunpacks were even considered

These lower hunting grounds always seem to have a healthy population of foxes, despite the fact that the fellpacks, and the driven shoots, hunt these regions. This is because of the abundance of wildlife that thrives in these lower dales, making food for Reynard plentiful. This means that, even though many foxes are taken from such locations, the springtime breeding will soon replenish stocks as foxes breed in larger numbers where food supplies are more plentiful.

Maybe the anti-hunting brigade should take notice of this. Foxes are hunted by fellpacks, fox shoots, terrier and lurchermen, in the lower dales of Cumbria, yet they continue to thrive; proof enough that hunting is not about destruction, but about maintaining a healthy population, taking out the old, the weak and the sick, which cuts down on the risk of infectious disease breaking out, and keeps numbers as low as possible for the sake of shepherds and farmers who have livestock to protect. Hunting can never be about destruction, or elimination. In fact, hunting is not really an accurate description. 'Countryside management' is a much better term that sums up exactly, what rural pursuits are about!

One of the main problems with hunting these lowlands where woodland and forestry flourish, usually covering large tracts of land, is that it is all too easy to lose touch with hounds as Reynard can run around these coverts for hours on end, very often keeping well ahead of the pack by using well worn pathways which have taken foxes to their feeding grounds for centuries. It is not unusual for a pack to change foxes while drawing through this type of landscape, which is difficult to say the least. Hounds will often split into two or three groups and hunt two or three foxes

Stan Mattinson with hounds in the low country.

at the same time which makes following even more difficult. Grisedale forest is one of the most difficult areas to hunt and listening for the baying of hounds is the only way to keep in touch in this situation, for viewing them, unless they run past closeby, is nigh on impossible. There are quite a number of thick woodlands at the head of Windermere and Reynard will often use these in order to put some distance betwixt himself and the oncoming pack.

The English Lake District is a place full of enchantment and natural beauty which is only enhanced by the severe weather conditions which can break out so quickly. Sudden storms break out up on the higher ground and these too can make life difficult for the hunter of the fox, though the weather has to be very severe before it succeeds in stopping hunting.

A tale of Patterdale terriers and a stormy day is now apt, I feel, though, at the time, these terriers were not known by this name. During his mastership of the Coniston Foxhounds, when Anthony Chapman hunted the pack, Logan was given a number of Patterdale terriers by Frank Buck, which he used with the hunt, and very successfully too. Chapman was impressed by these terriers from the Buck/Breay breeding programme and they did much good work for the Coniston pack.

It was a fine morning in autumn and hounds were taken out to Red screes where the first draw was to take place. Red screes stands above the Kirkstone pass and the reason for the name soon becomes obvious to all who travel up that way, for the rocks are of a delicate red shade. This is a good place to find foxes, however, but their efforts were thwarted by a sudden storm drifting over the mountain and making conditions impossible, so hounds were taken to a nearby farm where they waited for the storm to abate. Abate it did and so at last the hunting could begin. Chapman was keen to get going, for a fox had taken a cockerel from the farm and they were hoping to catch up with it and end its crimes before it returned for more.

Hounds were now loosed at Red screes and it wasn't long before they struck a line, though they flew around on a drifting scent for a while, wild with excitement, before finally settling and getting somewhere. The heavy rain and strong winds meant that the going was difficult, but, nevertheless, they stuck to their task and followed scent to some rocks where they found the remains of the cockerel which had been taken that night, thus they could be confident that they were following the line of the guilty party. This is important, for when hounds are called out to deal with a poultry, or a lamb, killing fox, they are there to deal with the culprit, not just any fox. If the culprit is not accounted for quickly, then more livestock will be taken. Logan took three of his terriers down to these rocks and entered Vic, an extremely game terrier of the Patterdale type.

Hounds and terriers were marking keenly, but were taken back a few paces in order to allow the fox to bolt. Vic soon began baying furiously, really getting stuck into his fox and, in the end, persuading him to take his chances above ground. He bolted at great speed and was away across the screes with such exact steps that hounds were quickly put to shame by the agility of this marvellous creature. However, once out onto the fells, hounds pressed him hard, that hard, in fact, that he didn't even try finding a place to ground at some of the vast borrans he headed for. Finally, finding the pack too close for comfort, he headed for deep heather and by now the pack were baffled, being stuck as to where the line led.

Fellhounds are experts at hunting in all types of weather

conditions and across all types of country, and so it wasn't long before Cruel, a superb bitch hound, was onto him, pushing him out and away behind a huge crag. Hounds quickly followed and another long hunt began, which ended with Reynard running to ground inside another huge borran at Dove Crag, a notoriously bad place in the Lakes.

Again, one of the terriers was put to ground and managed to bolt its fox, despite the fact that he was exhausted and reluctant to face that pack again. The followers could clearly see that the fox was getting to the end of his fight, but still he got out onto the high tops and was away, finally securing his brush when another bad storm broke out and made scenting conditions impossible. This hunt well illustrates the gameness of those terriers that were given to Robin Logan by Buck just after the Second World War. Patterdale terriers have a long history of working with the Coniston foxhounds, and continue to do so today, and they have proved themselves working some of the worst spots in the country.

I can remember one particularly bad storm that broke out while I was again following the famed Blencathra pack. I was up on the bleak felltops above Walla Crag, which overlooks Derwentwater, looking out for hounds who were busy hunting two foxes which they had roused from dense undergrowth, mainly gorse, at the foot of these huge, fear-inspiring crags. I watched as Derwentwater and Keswick were swamped by hard, driving rain. Where I was standing, and on the high tops across the vale, snow fell. It was light and it was blown off my clothes by the strong wind. And then it simply drifted away as quickly as it had arrived, across the broad sweeping moorland behind me and leaving a sea of blue above,with Skiddaw now more majestic than ever, covered in a fresh layer of snow. Down in the town and along the shores of Derwentwater, the hordes of tourists would no doubt be soaked to the skin by now, the shops and cafés full to bursting with people attempting to avoid the downpour. There are advantages to getting your boots on and getting out onto those high, rugged fells!

'Rugged', now there's a word which perfectly describes the landscape of the English Lake District. It is a wild, bleak, windswept land. It can even be chilly during the summer months out on the higher slopes, but it is bitterly cold during winter when the wind blows strong enough to blow you off your feet. It can be difficult to breathe in the face of such gales, impossible to hear

A meet of the Coniston foxhounds.

anything but the buffeting of the wind all around, your eyes watering as the icy blast blows into them. Weather conditions often combine to make following a fellpack incredibly difficult. But then, other days come along which make up for this; days of a crystal clarity which makes the seeing and hearing of hounds much easier, the going good as the frost firms up the ground underneath your feet.

Weather conditions can also make it difficult for the terrier which has to endure miles of walking before it is even required to go to ground. This is why many have a preference for really hard-coated terriers, but the truth is that terriers with woolly, open coats, coats that are considered as poor by most terriermen today, were extremely common in the fells during previous decades and, particularly in the Coniston country. In fact, some of the terriers found in the Lakes today are descended from these types and they too have this woolly, open coat. Steve Dawes, terrierman for the Coniston foxhounds, has terriers with this type of coat, as do several other fell-hunters, so maybe that harsh, tightly-knit jacket is not as important as many stress! My opinion is that woolly jackets stand up to the cold well enough, but persistent rain in extremely cold temperatures would test such a coat to the full. Once the rain penetrates such a jacket and the icy wind creeps through to flesh and bone, a terrier is going to suffer.

Mining has, for centuries, been an important trade in and around Cumbria (the English Lake District was once divided between Cumberland, Westmorland and Lancashire), providing much work for local people and boosting the local economy. This trade thrived in former times, alongside quarrying, for Lakeland stone and slate are very attractive indeed. This stone and slate is not only attractive, but is durable and waterproof and the commodity enjoyed great popularity at one time so great chunks of land, entire fellsides almost, have been hacked out of the landscape, leaving huge scars behind, though, strangely enough, these are not unpleasing to the eye in any way.

That great fellwalking artist, Alfred Wainwright, once said that nobody really minds the land being scarred by quarrying as this trade is essential to the Cumbrian economy and helps to keep youngsters in the area who find employment at such places. This also helps to keep the local traditions alive and well. Fellhunting is one such tradition, but it is much more than this. Hunting in the fells was begun by shepherds who tired of losing large numbers of lambs to foxes – and some shepherds can lose over thirty lambs during one springtime to predators – deciding to keep hounds which they fed and housed between them and brought together for hunting purposes whenever they could manage to do so. This method is known as 'trencher-fed'. One of the shepherds was appointed to hunt the pack and this system remained in Cumbria for hundreds of years. Indeed, especially during his earlier years, this is the system that John Peel used when hunting his hounds.

Peel would blow the gather on his horn before hunting began and his hounds would soon be with him. He obviously had set days on which he hunted and the shepherds and farmers would undoubtedly have loosed their hounds early on so that they were free to head off to meet their Huntsman, keen to get started. Peel's hounds were incredibly useful and would hunt all day. They were much slower than the present-day fellhounds and often took an age to rouse their fox, spending hours on end following a cold drag until they eventually unkennelled their quarry, or, as

Hounds heading for the higher fells.

very often happens in the fells, marked it to ground. Terriers were then used to bolt Reynard from his lair, very often inside a rocky laybrinth, though not always for dug-out rabbit holes are fairly common in the low country. And Peel spent quite a bit of his time hunting the low grounds, as opposed to the fells, for he was extremely keen on mounted hunting and had several fell ponies throughout his long and eventful life which he used for riding to hounds. True, he did ride even in the fell country, especially on the slopes of Skiddaw where much of his hunting took place, but very often the pony would have to be abandoned and Peel would then follow on foot. It is said that he caught hares, a creature he hunted when foxes were scarce, from the saddle, hanging off it in a sort of acrobatic act and 'lifting' them as they became exhausted.

What Peel's terriers looked like is impossible to say, for I can find no information concerning them, but they were undoubtedly a fairly rough and ready bunch similar in colour and type to the Lowther Castle strain which were being bred and worked long before Peel was born. These terriers were of a type which gave rise to Fell, Lakeland, Border and Yorkshire terriers, as well as other breeds such as the Patterdale terrier.

Peel is considered as the 'father' of fell-hunting, but this type of hunting had been going on for centuries. But the passion which Peel displayed for hunting on the fells was something new and this was certainly catching, for fell-hunting, during Peel's day, was suddenly elevated to something far more than a means of carrying out pest control for the sake of the hill shepherd's, for Peel was just as passionate about the social side of fox and hare-hunting, as he was about the hunt itself.

John Peel would begin his hunting at daybreak. A drag would soon be struck, on one of the better days anyway, for foxes were far less common at this time (the mid-eighteenth century to the mid-nineteenth century) and were not always found, hence the reason why Peel would then switch to a hare instead. These drags on a cold scent, left behind as a fox passed in the night, could last for hours, starting in the low country around Caldbeck, or some other village nearby, and continuing up onto the high places miles away, finally marking a fox to ground, or un-kennelling it at a crag, or a borran, or out of the bracken and deep heather which flourishes in this type of country.

Hounds would then hunt their quarry for a few more hours, for, as I have already stated, they were much slower than modern-day hounds, though in many ways they could stick to a difficult line with far more patience and determination. Peel's hounds caught less foxes in a season than do today's packs, but, again, that is because foxes were harder to come by in those days. Many a good hunt took place around Skiddaw and a few good sized foxes of around sixteen pounds were taken from this area, but Peel hunted a massive country which stretched to the Scottish Border and possibly beyond. He also hunted around Ullswater and no doubt covered the Borrowdale valley. Wordsworth's poetic Huntsman, Simon Lee, may well have been based on Peel. These two famous historical figures lived at the same time and Wordsworth would undoubtedly have come across Peel while out on one of his forays into fell country, and he certainly visited the villages and rural areas where Peel was becoming a legend at the time, so it seems likely that Wordsworth would im-mortalise such a character in one of his poems.

After hunting, Peel would retire to a country inn, hang the fox from the ceiling and toast its cunning and bravery over and over again. Some say that his 'benders' went on for as long as three days at a time, but this is most unlikely, for Peel dealt in fell ponies, like his father before him, and had hounds to feed at home. He was a poor man and could not employ staff to do these things for him, so it is not likely that he would settle in a pub and not return home for days on end. These celebrations were rather rowdy, however, and large quantities of ale were drunk as the singing and celebrating dragged on well into the night. Peel's hunting ponies knew their way about country, and they had to do, for many a night they would carry their Huntsman home along the pitch-black tracks which led from village to village. Hounds and terriers were probably bedded down at the nearest farm for the night and then loosed in the morning, easily making their way back to kennels unaided. Although they were trencher-fed for many years, during his later life, Peel kennelled hounds at his own farm.

John Peel was such a fanatical hunter that, on the morning of his son's funeral, a lad named Peter of whom he was very fond, he was called out to hunt down a goose-killing fox in the low country. He took hounds to the farm, took up the scent and eventually, after a long hunt, caught and killed his fox, returning to the churchyard where he threw the brush into the grave where his son had now been placed. In the fells, everything must wait, especially when a fox is abroad which has just killed livestock at one of the farms!

While on holiday in the Lake District, I got talking to an old chap in Ambleside who had lived there all his life. He told me about his days hunting with Joe Bowman, that famed Ullswater foxhounds' Huntsman, and I found those tales fascinating, especially of those rowdy nights which were often spent at The Kirkstone Pass Inn, then known as The Traveller's Rest, in fine John Peel fashion, the dead fox hanging from the ceiling while the hunters toasted its courage over and over. He also said that Bowman had told him Peel was cruel with his hounds. Whether this referred to neglect, giving some credence to tales of his three day benders, I suppose, or to him beating them, I do not know, but I am very sceptical.

Peel's hounds had a reputation as being some of the best working hounds in the country, able to stick to a cold drag for miles on end, for several hours at a time, and then they would burst their hearts for their Huntsman in order to catch their prey, the actual hunting lasting for a few hours more. Peel began at daybreak and his hounds were still hunting after dark in many cases, which would be nigh-on impossible for hounds that were not fit and well fed. Would hounds work so hard for a cruel master? I think it unlikely. Also, quite a number of keen hunting men, reputable men, hunted with Peel and surely they would not have done so had he been cruel with his pack. John Peel, as a master and a very successful Huntsman, was open to much back-biting and this is where these rumours could have originated. Of course, it is impossible to completely refute such charges, but I think it most unlikely that this was so. John Woodcock Graves was Peel's closest friend who wrote the famous *D'ye ken John Peel*, and I think it most unlikely that such a tribute would have been paid had he been cruel with hounds. Peel was, however, quite a poor man throughout his lifetime and it is possible that on some days he had nothing to feed his hounds and terriers, but that cannot be construed as neglect. Missing the odd day's feed would do nothing to harm his pack, though I am sure that such days

Fellhunting country.

were rare, as Peel had many farmer friends who would surely have sent him their fallen stock.

Whatever the terriers Peel used, they were certainly of game stock, as the country he hunted contains many deep and dangerous borran earths, the most likely place that a hunted fox would head for when hounds are getting a little too close for comfort. True, he hunted much of the low country where dug-out rabbit earths are common enough, but the majority of Peel's hunts, even though they began on lower ground where he could be mounted, soon ended up on the fells where following on horseback became impossible, and so much foot following was also carried out by Peel, with foxes earthing, or being found, inside borrans, or crag earths. Of course, in this type of country extremely game terriers would be needed, terriers no doubt similar in type to many of the fell terriers found in early photographs; the rootstock of modern fell and Patterdale terriers.

Some of these borran earths are so vast that more than one terrier is entered in order to make finding a much speedier process, for a terrier can take an age to locate its fox, which may keep moving around such an earth, giving its pursuer the run around and always keeping one step ahead of the game. Sometimes, in some of the larger borrans, up to four terriers may be entered at any one time, though this is rare, two being a more usual number. Hounds will search a borran above too, and they have such good noses and hearing that they are often well aware of the location of a fox, long before the terrier has found, or bolted it.

The English Lake District is certainly a place of great natural beauty, but its crags and its vast borrans, natural features of the landscape, make life incredibly difficult for hounds and terriers hunting there, though the activities of man have made life even more difficult, when it comes to carrying out fox control in such places. Although quarrying and mining have provided much employment to the local people of the fell country, these man-made obstacles present a real danger to the hound and terrier hunting over this type of ground. Quarrying has taken huge chunks out of fellsides and hounds have been known to fall over the edge when too close to a fleeing fox. The blasting also creates huge cracks in the rocks, deep crevices which are impossible to dig, where a terrier to ground is in danger of falling into them and being stuck there forever. Crags, a black bitch bred down from Frank Buck's terrier strain and typical of the harsh-coated black

Frank Buck with the Wensleydale harriers. Buck and Donald Sinclair re-formed this pack and Frank was foot-huntsman for many years.

terriers he bred during his later years, died in a quarry earth, no doubt after falling into a crevice which was created when blasting had occurred. We dug for days on end in an attempt to locate her, but never did.

Old mineshafts are another hazard in fell-hunting country. Crevice, a dog which often worked alongside Crags and of the same type, had proven himself a great finder in many huge rock earths and was a credit to the strain of terrier, now known as Patterdales, that Buck bred and worked throughout his long life, using them with several packs of hounds and supplying hunt terriers all over the north. I worked with Crevice on a number of occasions and once he had to be rescued from a deep rockpile on the edge of yet another quarry, after he had bottled up his fox in rather a tight spot. It took a few days, but eventually he was reached and pulled out of the earth. This rockpile had always been a difficult earth to work, it being extremely hard to dig and so deep that foxes usually would not bolt. This hole that had been dug at the deepest part of the rockpile was left open and from then on it became much easier to bolt foxes and I had some cracking hunts there from then on; bolting foxes with the terriers and coursing them with lurchers.

Crevice was a superb finder, a good bolter of foxes and a terrier who could finish his foe if it refused to 'vacate the premises'. He was also of a good stamp, a real eye-catching terrier, but, sadly, he met his end when put into a very deep mineshaft which always holds a fox or two. I have bolted several foxes from these shafts over the years and have had no problems whatsoever (I no longer work old mineshafts as the risk of losing a terrier in such a place is far too high, due to possible poison gasses etc.). Crevice was entered and was quickly onto his fox, but he was never seen again. Of course, putting a locator collar on a terrier working an old mine is pointless, for the fifteen foot maximum depth is surpassed in just a few seconds and so there is no way of digging a terrier out of earths of this nature. Some places are best avoided and it would have been better if Crevice's owner had done so. This tale well illustrates how a hard country can so easily see off such valiant, capable workers, and the fell country is one of the hardest and most hostile of countries any hunter can work in. Tales of lost terriers in such country are too numerous to mention in just one book!

The Cumbrian people are tough, to say the least, moulded by the landscape and the weather conditions that prevail in this county, but its hounds and especially its terriers are tougher still. It truly is a land of excelling beauty, of hounds and terriers of unsurpassed ability.

2

THE ORIGINAL
PATTERDALE TERRIER

Early fell types of terrier were a hotch-potch of differing shapes and sizes and most were woolly-coated specimens with plenty of leg and coming in all shades, though blue grizzle, red, tan and black and tan were the most common colours at that time. Black terriers, referred to as Patterdales these days, were not as common, though they were to be found throughout the Lakes during the nineteenth and early twentieth centuries. Roger Westmoreland states that black terriers have existed for decades in the Coniston hunt country and that these can be seen in early photographs of George Chapman who hunted the Coniston pack with much success and who was well known for breeding good working stock. Gary Middleton told me that the Lakes has always produced black terriers, but that these were far from common, in fact, when he was 'nobbut a lad' he can only recall there being two black terriers in the whole of the Patterdale district, which gives much ammunition to critics of today's so-called Patterdale teriers who will argue that the evidence shows that the modern Patterdale strains have virtually no connection with this part of the world, though it is only fair to say that the terriers bred and worked in this district have been of such quality, in a working sense more than because of looks, that most modern Fell and Patterdale terriers have at least some blood of these terriers running through their veins.

Middleton, a very knowledgeable man concerning Fell terriers of the past hundred years or so, states that most of the terriers found in Patterdale and throughout the Ullswater hunt country in fact, were of obvious Bedlington ancestry, carrying the silky top-knot and very often the blue colouring in their coats. He went on to say that Sid Wilkinson's bitch Nettle, a superb worker who saw much service with the Ullswater hounds, displayed

The Coniston pack heading for the fells.

Bedlington terrier ancestry. He said that if Sid allowed the coat to grow the silky top-knot and the blue colouring would eventually appear, stripping the coat out a couple of times a year being the only way to prevent this from happening. Nettle was descended from Arthur Irving's Robin; a very typey terrier who worked as well as he looked. Middleton says that this terrier was descended from Fell types with much Bedlington blood in their veins which were polished up with Fox terrier blood. Robin was used on a number of terriers and Sid and Joe Wilkinson's strain could be traced back to this dog.

Roger Westmoreland confirms that Bedlington blood was apparent in many Fell types, but he also stated that Irish immigrants brought terriers with them from their native home-land and that these too entered into the old Fell strains. A look at old fell-hunting photographs will soon confirm this, for terriers of Irish terrier descent are obvious. Albert Benson's Red Ike, for instance, a terrier worked very successfully by Anthony

23

Chapman at the Coniston hunt, was a terrier which was obviously bred from the dogs brought to the Lakes by those immigrants. Irish Wheaten types were also found throughout the Lakes during the later nineteenth and early twentieth centuries and these can clearly be seen in old photos. When Irish terriers were first exhibited in their homeland, they came in all different shapes and sizes, some resembling Scottish terriers, others Bedlingtons, while some were quite typey red and black and tan terriers. It was just such stock that arrived in the Lake District and went into the mixed brew that eventually gave rise to the Fell strains of today, including the strains now known, however inaccurately, as Patterdale terriers. Just take a look at the terrier Kelly, in Clapham's fascinating account of Cumbrian hunting, *Foxhunting On The Lakeland Fells*, as this terrier would easily pass for one of the unregistered Wheaten terriers still worked in some parts of Ireland by a dedicated few.

Bedlingtons were easily available to Lake District hunters as travellers often came to such districts plying their trade. Irish farm workers also arrived on our shores each year looking for seasonal work and these too would undoubtedly bring their terriers with them, many being similar in type to the old fell strains, though their owners would vigorously deny that they had anything to do with English breeds. These terriers, great all-round workers which could tackle vermin and herd cattle and sheep, would also have gone into the mix and so, by the early part of the twentieth century, there was an odd mixture of different types; some with Bedlington ancestry, some displaying Wheaten and Irish terrier ancestry, some with obvious Fox terrier blood, while others resembled the old strains of Scottish and Cairn terriers. They were a rough and ready bunch, but there were also some superb typey animals to be found, especially along the west coast where Irish terrier blood improved type, but also in other parts of Cumbria.

Two Buck-bred terriers with short legs and square, powerful heads which, in my view, display a hint of Scottish terrier blood.

Middleton stated that Fox terrier blood was used to improve type in many of the

Bedlington terrier type fell terriers and Jim Dalton, Huntsman for many years of the Blencathra foxhounds and still held in high regard by many of the older generation of fell-hunters in this part of the Lakes, was one of those who used this outcross, for he was a real fan of working Fox terriers and had easy access to some of the best in the country.

A Fox terrier named Lill Foiler was owned and worked by the master of the Carlisle and District Otterhounds which were kennelled just up the road from where Dalton lived. This bitch was descended from such notable terriers as Parson Russell's famous Tip, an extraordinary worker which ran with hounds for several seasons and did much good work for the Parson, and Russell's superb worker Vic, a terrier with a wonderful finding ability both below and above ground. This terrier found foxes deep in covert where hounds had failed on quite a number of occasions and was one of the Parson's best and most reliable workers. If hounds had drawn blank at a covert Russell was sure should hold, Vic would be sent into it and on many occasions he would find. With breeding such as this, Lill must have been a superb terrier and I have no doubts at all that Dalton would have brought such easily accessible blood into his own fell terrier strain, for Dalton certainly followed this pack of otterhounds and would have known hunt staff and masters very well indeed, for it is also likely that they followed the Blencathra during the winter months when otters were enjoying the closed season.

Lill and her offspring were regarded as the same general type which the Parson bred and worked; typey terriers which were first and foremost workers, though they also did very well in the showring too. Obviously, no matter how typey such dogs were, or how successful they were in the showring, working qualities came first for most breeders at that time and Dalton was no exception. His terriers had a reputation as being some of the gamest in the fells and working qualities suffered not at all by the inclusion of Fox terrier blood, for then, unlike today, sadly, the vast majority of Fox terriers were still worked regularly to fox, badger and otter, and one can easily understand why these old fell-huntsmen turned to such blood to improve the terriers they were breeding. But it wasn't just about type, for early fell terriers often had poor coats, which meant they suffered quite a bit during the harsh midwinter. Huntsmen such as Dalton saw in the Fox terrier a way of improving coat in their own hunt terriers.

Many early fell terriers also had quite weak heads and short, stumpy legs. The addition of Fox terrier, and, in many cases, Irish terrier blood, did much to improve these faults, producing much tighter, harsher jackets, bigger and stronger heads and good length of leg. These improved strains began to produce terriers that were collected by show enthusiasts and the pedigree Lakeland terrier soon emerged after better type had been fixed, though many of the older strains continued to be kept and worked and some have even survived down to today. For instance, the type of terriers kept by Steve Dawes of the Coniston hunt are typical of the old strains which have been bred and worked in this region for many decades, displaying obvious Bedlington terrier influence. Tag, for example, a very game terrier which served for many seasons with this hunt, a terrier I saw in action myself as it happens, is a replica of many old strains of fell terrier which were once common throughout the Lakes country, including in the district of Patterdale.

The Melbreak hunt, under the influence of one of its finest Huntsmen, Willie Irving, produced typey terriers which were obviously improved by Fox and Irish terrier blood being added to Bedlington blooded fell types, but the terriers being bred at the Ullswater, and, more to the point, in the Ullswater hunt country by breeders such as Fred and Anthony Barker, and Sid and Joe Wilkinson, were also vastly superior in type to the old strains which often had poor coats. The Wilkinson terriers were bred down from Braithwaite Wilson's working stock which he considered to be free of Bedlington blood and which were in all probability bred out of good class Irish stock that had been mated to local fell strains, for Wilson's earth dogs were leggy, hard-coated terriers that, I believe, displayed Irish terrier somewhere in their make-up, or possibly even Fox terrier. Kitty Farrer, a committee member of the Ullswater foxhounds for many years and a friend of Wilson's, used Dalton's terriers to spice up his own breeding programme, so maybe Wilson did the same. Whatever the blood used, it was obvious that his terriers were only very distantly related to the old Bedlington-influenced bloodlines (few fell terriers have not at some time had Bedlington blood in their ancestry).

Wilson referred to his stock as Patterdale terriers, but my research highlights that this term was never used to indicate a separate breed, or even a separate strain of fell terrier. Both Westmoreland and Middleton state that there was no such thing as a Patterdale terrier in breed terms, for they were known simply as fell terriers, or, when Middleton was a lad, as Lakelands. This term was given to the pedigree Lakeland when Kennel Club recognition was granted in 1921. The name was already used in some districts for the improved strains of fell terrier in particular, well before this time, especially since a club was formed in Keswick in 1912 when the breeding of the new type was better organised in order to gain entry into the Kennel Club. Gary mentioned that most fell terrier owners, especially in the Patterdale district where he spent much of his hunting life with such worthy characters as Anthony Barker and Sid Wilkinson, two of the most important fell terrier breeders in Cumbrian history and whose bloodlines Middleton has continued to this day, referred to their terriers as Lakelands.

The term Patterdale terrier was used to imply the district where the terrier had been bred, though it is true to say that terriers bred

Nuttall's Shamrock (Shammy) served two seasons with Eskdale and Ennerdale foxhounds.

throughout the Ullswater country were often known as Patterdales, despite the fact that this is only a tiny village and that few terriermen have ever lived there, the two most noteworthy being Fred and Anthony Barker. Middleton mentioned that the original Patterdale terrier was very much of the type that his strain now produces. He said that many bad losers at working terrier shows often accuse him of putting pedigree Lakelands onto his bitches in order to improve type. But, as he says, it was the pedigree Lakeland that arose from dogs of this type in the first place, so why would he have need of resorting to such a cross when he breeds a type of terrier which looks and often works as well as the original Lakeland that had come about by using Fox and Irish terrier blood, which was added to the old mongrelly fell types that displayed much Bedlington about them? True, working ability has suffered on some of the terriers bred out of Middleton stock these days, for many just exhibit their charges and do not work them at all, but, as Wendy Pinkney states, 'Middleton's terriers were once among the best in the world'. Wendy used a Middleton bred terrier, Ben, owned by Brian Fleming, to bring into her own fell strain and she had no qualms about doing so, such is the reputation of the older strains of Middleton bred terriers. And no wonder, for the terriers bred and worked in and around Patterdale during former times were unbeatable as workers; something that the modern Patterdale has in common with the original strains.

Roger Westmoreland went on to say that Patterdale terriers were named as such because of the area where they were bred, just as terriers from Kendal were called 'Kendal terriers', those from Grasmere, 'Grasmere terriers', from Carlisle, 'Carlisle terriers', and so on and so forth. Do not forget, in the old days communities were much more isolated than they are today. Easy access to fast transport has changed many things, including the way in which terriers are bred. Each hunt country would have its different top working dog terriers at stud; those that had proven themselves as superb workers, a cut above the rest. These stud dogs, numbering only a few in each district, would serve many of the bitches in that area and so would stamp their type on the resultant offspring, thus the reason for each district producing its own type of terrier.

It is the same story throughout the country but especially in northern parts. The Scottish Highlands for instance, produced different types in different districts. On the eastern side were terriers that gave rise to the Scottish terrier, while to the west the Cairn, its white counterpart, the West Highland, and the Skye terrier were all emerging, despite the fact that they were all from the same basic rootstock. In the Rothbury forest area terriers were emerging which gave rise to the Bedlington, the Dandie Dinmont and the Border terrier, again all rising from the same rootstock; rough and ready tykes of all different colours and types. The early stock of terriers in these districts had their own names and were different in type and colour, but all have been taken into the breeding programmes which have given rise to these three breeds.

The Rothbury terrier gave rise to the Bedlington which, as *Hutchinson's Dog Encyclopedia* explains, was once known as the Northumberland fox terrier, while the Reedwater, or Coquetdale terrier gave rise to the Border. The Redesdale terrier was another type bred in this area which lost ground to more typey stock and eventually disappeared, though the bloodlines of old terriers such as this have undoubtedly entered into the stock which gave rise to these modern breeds. The Redesdale was an all-white terrier which was similar in type to the Lowther Castle strain that were typical of early fell types. It is a fascinating story, but one difficult to fathom. What is certain, however, is that there was no such thing as a Patterdale terrier in terms of a separate breed. Patterdales were simply fell terriers which were bred in and around that area.

If one looks at the pedigree of Breay and Buck's strain, the ancestors of what are known today as Patterdale terriers, then this way of naming terriers becomes obvious to the reader. On page 107 of Plummer's *The Fell Terrier*, there are references to 'Coniston dog' and 'Cockermouth dog', confirming what Westmoreland said about terriers being named after the districts where they were bred and worked, the truth being that they were all just fell types which had slight differences in type depending on the district from whence they came. So references to early Patterdale terriers are simply implying the district they were bred in, rather than meaning a separate breed. The truth is, the terriers produced in the Patterdale area were nothing like the terriers which have been given that name today.

Middleton says that there have always been smooth-coated terriers in the Lakes and photographic evidence certainly backs up what he says. Fox terriers were used extensively on early fell strains in order to breed away from the poor coated Bedlington types that were all too common in the fells during the latter part of the nineteenth century and the early part of the twentieth, and this cross undoubtedly produced smooth coats as well as tighter, harsher coats so beloved by fell-hunters such as Wilson, Barker and Middleton. Douglas Paisley, of the Blencathra foxhounds, used Fox terrier blood to improve his fell types, possibly even using much the same blood as Dalton had done earlier, and his strain produced the odd smooth-coated terrier, known as 'Slape-coated' in the fells. But another cross also brought in this smooth coat. Gary mentioned that a lot of the smooth-coated fell types that were knocking about when he was a small boy, carried quite a bit of Bull terrier blood in their veins, the fell-hunters regarding them as mongrel terriers, rather than Lakelands. Nevertheless, as Gary stated, these Bull-influenced terriers were incredibly game and undoubtedly entered many of the fell strains which, in some

Danny Sykes' superb worker, Brick; a dog bred out of Buck/Breay stock.

cases, were in dire need of outcross blood in order to improve both courage and bone structure, for many early fell types had poor heads and weak jaws. Fox terriers of a hundred years ago carried quite a bit of Bull terrier blood, and this is obvious by the size and strength of some of the heads on these early terriers, and this cross undoubtedly helped to improve bone structure in early fell strains, but the Bull/fell terrier crosses also played their part in improving bone and courage in many of the old strains which were first and foremost workers.

Because of the nature of the terrain, terriers are needed that are capable of closing with their fox and finishing it below ground, should it refuse to bolt. In gentler hunt countries, foxes can usually be dug out if the landowner requires it, but in the fells foxes will often head to places that are impossible to dig. A fox holed-up in a huge borran earth, after killing livestock at a farm down in the lower dales, must be accounted for. A terrier may be entered which will stand back and bay at its fox, thus bolting it to hounds, though most likely a harder terrier will be put in, in the hopes that it will close with its quarry and deal with it below ground, for a bolted fox has a real chance of making good its escape, while a fox to ground with a hard terrier is sure to be dealt with and its crimes ended. My belief is that Bull terrier blood has played a part in creating such hard stock, for the old fighting terriers descended from early Bulldogs were easily accessible to the older generation of fell-hunters.

These terriers were often kept by miners who used them, not only for dog fighting, but for badger baiting and as seizure dogs at the end of fox and badger digs. These terrier types were far more agile than today's Staffordshire Bull terrier, for they were lighter and smaller and incredibly game. The smooth-coated fell terriers which displayed Bull terrier blood in their make-up during Gary's youth, and well before that time, were undoubtedly descended from such fighting dogs which entered fell strains in order to produce fox killers and much stronger-boned offspring with jaws like vices.

Bradley's Rip (page 112 *The Fell Terrier*) was typical of the type Gary mentioned which have been in the fells for decades, for this terrier was obviously descended from these fighting Bull terriers which were used to improve many strains of terrier, including fells and, a little later, Border terriers which also suffered from weak heads and poor, snipey jaws. Plummer mentions that Rip served numerous bitches in the north, indicating that he was a

Mist (*left*) out of Barry Wild's black stuff. Fell (*right*) bred by Wendy Pinkney.

superb worker, and so this fighting Bull terrier blood entered many strains of Fell through this dog.

Border terriers share the same common ancestry as the fell terrier, but, as I said, many of the early types had very poor heads and jaws. Anyone who looks at the massive head of Bradley's Rip, and the modern Border terrier, cannot help but conclude that Bull terrier blood, the more agile and slender type used by miners decades ago, was indeed responsible for the improvements brought about by such a cross. I believe that Bedlington blooded fell types, crossed with these old fighting terriers and Irish terriers (the Border displays the same love of water as the Irish terrier, not to mention a similar harsh, tight jacket when it is stripped out), is the mix that has given rise to the modern Border terrier which is still a very useful working dog.

Fox predation can take a heavy toll on the livelihoods of Lakeland shepherds and this is the reason for fell-hunting's existence. During the days of Peel, and well before that time, foxes were hunted as vermin and there was far less emphasis on the social side, or on the sporting element, than there is today. Fell-hunting continues to be a very useful form of fox control, but it is far easier than it was in the old days. Life for hounds, terriers and

Huntsmen is, it is true, easier in these modern times, but still, this continues to be a hard way of life and it is just as bad now, as it ever was, when one gets caught out in a storm on those exposed fells.

The old time fellpack Huntsman had to be as hard as iron. Modern conveniences were not available and he would be up well before the break of day, cleaning out the kennels and seeing to those hounds and terriers which would not be going out that day. And then, well before the start of hunting, he would gather his pack and couple his terriers and set off on what was often a very long walk, just to get to the meet itself, before any hunting had begun. His day would already be a long one, despite the fact that not one cast had yet been made. Once at the meet, the hounds would be taken off for the first draw and hopefully the day's action would soon begin. In those days hounds were much slower at their work and, like those hunted by Peel and his associates, would take an age to work out a cold drag. In the shires hounds are taken to and from covert until they find a fox skulking inside one of them, but in the fells there are very few coverts and so hounds must find the drag of a fox which has passed-by during the early hours and stick to that drag until they either unkennel their quarry, or mark it to ground. Deep heather, a ledge on a crag, bracken and reedbeds are the most likely places to find above ground, borran earths, rather than dug-out rabbit holes, the favoured place below ground, though dug-out rabbit holes are sometimes used by foxes inhabiting the lower dales. The true fell fox, however, usually holes-up in some rocky laybrinth high on the fellside.

After maybe a couple of hours of following a cold drag and methodically working out the line, a find is at last accomplished and the real hunting can begin. When one considers the nature of such hunting, the cold drag being one of the most important facets of fell-hunting in particular, it is easy to appreciate why Huntsmen found true hunting hounds absolutely essential. Hounds, for instance, which hunt 'heelway', that is, following the scent from whence the fox came, rather than in the direction it was going, are of no use to a fellpack Huntsman who must urge his pack on in order that their quarry can be found as soon as possible. Obviously, hounds which mislead their fellow pack members and who take them 'backtracking' will not find at all and much time and energy will be wasted, so it is vital that hounds hunt true.

It is amazing to see how a pack of hounds can so easily be misled by one or two members which show a tendency to hunt 'heelway'. When I was out with the Lunesdale foxhounds one of the hounds, after a fox had broke cover at last, having run the pack around the huge pheasant woods near Milnthorpe for most of the day, began hunting backwards and the rest of the pack followed. Paul Whitehead, the current Huntsman, firmly put them right after much effort and very soon the more experienced hounds began turning away and heading off in the right direction, with the whole pack eventually following. It took some effort on Paul's part to put them right and young hounds will quickly learn not to backtrack on scent when a Huntsman diligently corrects this fault, though some hounds do not learn and must be removed from the pack lest they lead others into similar 'illegal' endeavours. One can imagine the time and energy that would be lost out on those bleak fells if a pack hunted the wrong way.

Once a find has been accomplished the pack will follow in the wake of their eagerly sought fox and the Huntsman and Whip must follow as best they can. While the cold drag has been painstakingly worked out over maybe a couple of hours or so, the Huntsman, apart from a few encouraging words, will have pretty much left them to their own devices and this is most important, for fellhounds, once they have found, will be away from their Huntsman in minutes, if not seconds, and so they must be able to work unaided. Hounds which constantly look to their Huntsman for assistance, as a shire pack will when the going gets tough, are nigh-on useless for hunting on the fells. When a check comes, as it often will during the course of an average hunt, a pack must think for itself and cast in the most obvious places until scent is once more taken up. The more experienced members of a pack, old hands at this game, will take over at such checks and they are not usually wrong when they make a cast. The younger team members learn from such experiences and one day will be more than capable of hunting unaided too.

Keeping in touch with hounds, especially in the old days, was incredibly difficult and the best way of going about it, as is still the case today, is to head out onto the high tops and hope for the best. The trouble is, even when one can clearly hear the pack, it is not always possible to see them, for they could be in the next valley or hunting through a dense mist. Sometimes a Huntsman would lose his pack altogether and not see them again until the end of the day. This was quite a rare occurrence though, but it did happen and Huntsmen have even been known to go in the completely opposite direction to the pack.

When hounds quickly disappeared in this manner, usually on a screaming scent, the old time fell-hunters had to use instinct in order to find their pack. As I have said, that instinct occasionally led them astray and chancing upon a follower heading for home late in the afternoon may have been the only hope of discovering their whereabouts, or maybe an old hound, if the pack had run their quarry to ground and were now eagerly marking, would go in search of their Huntsman and lead him back to his pack. Hill farmers working out on the fells would also help to put a Huntsman right if he had totally lost contact with his pack. On rare occasions, hounds wouldn't be found at all, but they would make their way back to kennels of their own accord, or to the place where they were 'walked' during the summer off-season, and so the Huntsman wasn't too worried, though he much preferred to have all his hounds safe in kennels at the end of each hunting day. Even today, with all of those modern conveniences such as cars and CB radios, some hounds are still left out, but, again, will usually make their way back to kennels, or the place where they are walked. Nowadays, however, a hound making its way home at night is in danger of being knocked over by a motorist, something which never troubled the old time fellpack.

Of course, a hunting day could last well into the night, especially if there was a full moon and the Huntsman was able to get across country more easily in the dark, finally culminating in a kill, or a fox being run to ground in a bad place, but the working day of the old time fell Huntsman was still not over, for hounds, once back in kennel, had to be fed and watered and any wounds seen to before bedding them down at last. By the time the Huntsman got around to feeding and 'watering' himself, it could be gone midnight, so one can easily imagine what a hard and demanding life this was.

Each fellpack covers quite a large area that has to be hunted on a fairly regular basis in order to keep the hill shepherds happy, for fell-hunting is about predator control first and foremost, and always has been. In the old days there were no cars or wagons which could get them to a distant meet. The day before hunting, therefore, hounds had to be taken to the area where the meet was to take place and they were kept overnight at a local farm, where there was also a bed for the Huntsman. If not too distant, then hounds would be taken along from kennels on the same morning of the meet, usually walking many miles before hunting began, but some areas were just too far away and so the travelling was done during the previous day. Hounds and their Huntsman would then stay at the farm for that week, along with the Whip if the pack employed one, though, as with today, funds didn't always allow this, usually from Monday night through to Sunday morning when the pack would be taken back to kennel, or, in some cases, on to another farm in yet another distant district to be hunted for that week. Huntsman, Whip, hounds and terriers could be away from kennels for upwards of three or four weeks at a time. This truly was a hard life.

Nowadays, Huntsman and Whip, together with hounds and terriers, travel to the meet in a comfortable vehicle with a trailer hooked up to it, so, apart from getting the pack ready and loading them for the journey, there is little energy expended before the hunting actually begins. Some farmers still like to have hounds kennelled at their farm for the week when their valley

A terrier must stay until dug out. Patterdales are notorious stayers.

will be hunted, but Huntsman and Whip can now travel back to kennels and their families where injured hounds and terriers are cared for. CB radios now make keeping in touch with hounds far easier.

Followers are scattered about all over the felltops and there are usually plenty of car followers down in the valley bottoms, so it is nigh-on impossible to lose touch with the pack, though, of course, this does happen on occasion, but a car follower will usually find them in a relatively short time. If hounds do get away to a distant spot, then the Huntsman and Whip can get a lift with a car follower who will drop them off at the nearest place to where hounds were last seen. In the old days this was impossible and hunt servants had no choice but to walk and keep walking, usually for hours on end without sight or sound of the pack. If a 'come-a-courting' dog fox was encountered, usually in January, or around that time, a fox referred to as 'straight-necked' in the fells, and he decided to head back to his own country, then some incredibly long hunts ensued.

I was once out with the Coniston hunt and a courting dog fox was encountered above the small village of Troutbeck. This was a game fox indeed for he took the pack across miles of fell and dale, passing the hunt kennels at Ambleside and heading for the fells above Rydal park. He crossed Heron pike and then finished up in the Ullswater country where hounds finally lost him at Black Crag above Patterdale. This was a tremendously long hunt and the hunt servants managed to keep in touch only with the aid of car followers. As I have said, this commodity was not available in the old days and the hunt servants relied on an intimate knowledge of the country, a sound knowledge of the hunted beast and an instinct borne of vast experience; instinct that rarely led them astray, in order to keep in touch with hounds.

Once hounds were found, or called in by blowing 'the gather' on the horn, it was time to head back to kennels, or, in some cases, especially if they were out very late, perhaps after digging a fox out of a difficult rock earth, to the nearest farm which would have somewhere to house both hunt servants and their pack. The fell Huntsman of today is rarely more than forty-five minutes away from kennels and, no matter where the pack finish their day, a keen follower will bring the hunt wagon to the nearest spot. So, in many ways, hunt service in the fells is much easier than in previous times, but then again much more time and energy can be put into the hunting itself, rather than into just getting to and from meets. This being said, walking on the fells and battling through unbelievably bad weather conditions, and actually catching those foxes, is just as difficult!

Fred Barker was one of those old time fell-huntsmen who hunted a pack of fellhounds in Cumbria and among the bleak, wild and windswept North Pennines, a truly difficult country for hounds and terriers to work successfully. Barker, however, was made of stern stuff and he was a passionate fox-hunter and keen badger digger at a time when this practice was both legal and respectable. He hunted the original Pennine foxhounds, which were trencher-fed. In fact, Barker based his hunting very much on that of Peel, who had become a legend by this time, even enjoying a god-like status among many hunting communities, and there are many similarities 'twixt Barker and Peel.

Just like Peel in his earlier days, Barker, on pre-arranged hunting days, would blow 'the gather' on his horn early in the morning and the rest of the pack would soon be with him. Barker also used ponies to travel to and from meets and, undoubtedly, for getting across country when hunting the lowlands, though much of Barker's hunting was carried out on the high swell of the Pennines. He was very keen on hounds and was an expert at hunting them, but he was also just as keen on his terriers and must be regarded as one of the most important fell-hunting terriermen of all time, a man who did much to influence fell terrier breeding and whose bloodlines continue to run strong in both modern fell terriers and modern Patterdales.

Barker's most famous terrier was his red dog, 'Chowt'-faced Rock; an incredible worker who had proved his worth hunting some of the most difficult country in the Kingdom which contains earths ranging from dug-out rabbit holes to vast rockpiles and borrans. Rock was a strong, chunky terrier with a large, very powerful head, which displayed slight Bull terrier influence and more than a little Irish terrier blood about him. Where this terrier came from is a mystery to say the least, but it is likely that Fred Barker had bred him out of his own strain. Whether or not Bowman had any influence on this breeding programme is a debatable point, but one thing is certain and that is that Fred Barker bred his terriers with as much enthusiasm as he did his hounds and so it is very likely that this terrier was of his own strain, though the origins of the strain may well have come from Bowman in the first place, for Barker certainly knew him long before moving to Patterdale in the early 1920s.

The low country where plentiful cover gives shelter to a large number of foxes.

The Ullswater country bordered with that of the Pennine foxhounds and no doubt these two great Huntsmen had met on several occasions at shows which continue to be staged in this part of the world throughout the summer months. Bowman certainly kept and bred extremely game terriers and I have no doubt that Barker would have had no reserves about starting his terrier strain from such top class workers. Bowman obtained much of his stock from miners and local farmers, true, but he also bred his own stock and put them out at walk, getting the gamest back and using them frequently with the Ullswater pack.

'Chowt'-faced Rock was incredibly game and was more than capable of killing any fox which refused to bolt, his huge head and steel-trap jaws enabling him to face even the toughest of hill foxes. Barker's strain, in fact, built up such a good reputation that its worth was appreciated even at the other end of the country. Fred's strain needed outcross blood and some of the gamest terriers at that time were to be found at badger digging clubs. The Ilfracombe badger digging club, no doubt after having hunted with the Pennine hunt, were so impressed with Barker's strain that, on deciding that they too needed outcross blood, arranged to swap two of their Fox terrier types for some of Barker's fell types, despite the fact that these fells were coloured, as opposed to the club's white-bodied terriers. Barker's strain, however, carried the genes of white terriers, no doubt from a Fox terrier influence which was common among fell terriers even as early as the latter part of the nineteenth century, and his dog Rock had a large white blaze on his chest.

Of course, as I stated earlier, Fox terriers were bred and worked in fairly large numbers at the Carlisle and District Otterhounds, as well as at other places throughout the fells. Barker lived at Ousby (a small village on the outskirts of Penrith, at the foot of the Northern Pennines where the hunter gets the feeling of being on the summits of England), before moving to the Ullswater country during the early 1920s. This was inside the country hunted by this famous otter-hunting pack and he no doubt followed them whenever he could manage a day off during the busy summer months (Fred Barker was a hill shepherd, a trade that his son, Anthony, later took up), and he had easy access to game white-bodied terriers, some of which were descended from the dogs of Parson John Russell himself.

I firmly believe that it was such terriers that greatly influenced the breeding programmes of fell terrier enthusiasts such as Dalton and Douglas Paisley, and possibly Fred Barker and even Joe Bowman, for many of Bowman's coloured terriers threw the occasional white puppy. Bowman's Lill was one of these and I cannot help but wonder if this famous brood bitch, a superb worker, was descended from Lill Foiler which was bred out of the Parson's stock and who saw much service at the Carlisle kennels; a bitch who in turn bred some incredibly good-looking and working earth dogs. The Carlisle pack hunted much of the Ullswater country and Bowman would have known masters and hunt servants well, so there is every reason to believe that this is so. The Fox terriers bred and worked at the Carlisle and District Kennels had great reputations as workers and I have absolutely no doubts at all that these terriers were extensively used by the passionate hunters of the fells, for game terriers mean everything in this part of the world and nothing less is acceptable.

A bitch named Corby well illustrates the courage and abilities

Fell and Mist, hard working terriers bred down from Buck/Breay stock.

of some of the fell terriers which have had a great influence on modern bloodlines. This fell terrier bitch was actually owned by Lord Decies, but she was loaned to Joe Bowman who worked her enthusiastically and no doubt bred much of his future stock from this bitch.

The Ullswater foxhounds hunt an incredibly wild and barren landscape where weather conditions can suddenly turn very nasty indeed; from a sunny, frosty morning, to raging winds and snow blizzards by early afternoon, and hunters can so easily be caught out in such weather. This has happened to me on more than one occasion, but the worst storm I have ever been caught out in was when I was crossing a bleak moor in order to work a few rockpiles on the other side of it where foxes frequently earth'd. It wasn't a particularly fine day to begin with, but as I started to cross the moor a sudden storm blew in and a snow blizzard obliterated everything from view, the icy wind making it almost impossible for me to keep my head up as it blew directly into my face.

I knew this country well and had crossed the moor a thousand times before, but the heavy blanket of snow descending upon me was disorientating to say the least and it wasn't long before I hadn't a clue where I was. As the storm pressed in on me, I scanned the horizon and marked the spot where, in the distance, I could just see the sharp, jutting crest of the rockpiles I was heading for, marking the spot before the view was completely wiped out in a matter of seconds and hoping that I had not turned aside from my course as I battled on through the dense blizzard. Put yourself out on the high mountaintops with their sudden-drop crags all over the place and one can easily see how dangerous such conditions are up in the fell country. I made it across that moor with my terriers and lurchers and, sure enough, found a fox skulking in a large rockpile which was quickly evicted by two of my terriers, but had I been on a mountain at the time, I think I would have stayed put until the blizzard began to lift.

Despite these conditions, the Ullswater pack have always been a very good unit and they do a superb job of controlling fox numbers in that part of the world. And there are plenty of foxes in the Ullswater country. By the spring of 1923, the year before

Mist checking out a rabbit hole.

Bowman finally retired from hunt service after many years at the helm, having first begun hunting this pack in 1879 and holding that post, apart from a brief period during the First World War, until 1924; the hounds had accounted for over eighty foxes, a remarkable record indeed.

On one of his innumerable hunts, hounds had hunted, a big, game fell fox, across the harsh and difficult terrain of the high mountains which tower above Ullswater, and eventually Reynard was forced to seek sanctuary inside a big, rough spot, below a crag close to the lake. During those days a lot of terriers ran with hounds and Corby soon followed her fox into this large borran earth. This rocky den proved a difficult place indeed and, despite the fact that Corby was now really at her fox, having been hard-pressed by the fleet Ullswater pack, it refused to bolt, preferring to take its chances with the terrier instead. Foxes will often do this, especially where they find themselves in a good, commanding position, usually on a ledge, or on an uphill slope from where it can do much damage to a game terrier. Many good terriers will fail to shift a fox, or kill it in such circumstances, but then there are the elite class of terrier which are incredibly useful in this situation. Corby was of that elite class and she was not going to be outwitted by her fox.

It would have been better for that fox if it had bolted, for Corby proved extremely game and was undoubtedly one of the best terriers ever to have seen service at the Ullswater, or any other fellpack for that matter. A long dig into this borran now began and the going was so difficult and laborious that it took over twenty hours to finally reach the terrier who had stuck at her quarry without flinching. After clearing a space around the terrier and finally lifting her out of the earth, the diggers came upon the dead bodies of three large foxes which, when weighed later on, all scaled in at over twenty pounds each – an incredible feat for a terrier weighing in at around fifteen to seventeen pounds and being about the same size, possibly even smaller, than an average fox. She was in a bad state however, as you can imagine, and so was immediately taken back to kennels for treatment.

Bowman had quite a number of terriers that were capable of such feats throughout his long and eventful life and I am certain that he would have bred from such terriers and kept their precious bloodlines alive. There are no doubts that Bowman had many terriers on loan, as was the case with Corby, but it is also a certainty that such terriers would have been bred from on a number of occasions, the puppies put out at walk and the best of the bunch taken into hunt service back at the kennels; a system used by all the fellpack Huntsmen.

Fury (*Reminiscences of Joe Bowman – The miner's story*) was another Ullswater, or Patterdale terrier, that was capable of such feats and I did wonder if Corby and this terrier were one and the same. Corby could have been the pet name given by Lord Decies, while Fury was her kennel name whilst at hunt service, but there are significant points which would rule this out. Firstly, Fury entered a borran earth out on the fells, while Corby was put into a borran below a crag directly above Ullswater. Fury emerged after killing three foxes, while Corby was trapped, possibly by a corpse blocking her exit; not an unknown occurrence when working rock earths in particular, only being dug out after over twenty hours of hard graft.

It seems that Bowman actually owned Fury, for he gave her to Harold Watson (*The Fell Terrier*, D.B.Plummer, page 222) when he retired from hunt service in 1924, while Corby, as we have seen, was only on loan. The final clincher, however, which proves beyond doubt that these were two separate terriers is the fact that Corby served at the Ullswater during the late 1890s and early 1900s, while Fury, as we have seen, served during the 1920s, at the end of Bowman's distinguished career. That Fury was descended from Corby is impossible to prove, though it is very likely, for Huntsmen value highly the precious bloodlines of terriers of such extraordinary abilities. That a Huntsman is blessed once with a terrier of such abilities is something to be eternally grateful for, but to be blessed with quite a few in one's lifetime, as Bowman was, is amazing. These original Patterdale terriers, referred to in this way by hunters such as Wilson and Bowman, often produced terriers of such abilities.

Rumour has it that Fred Barker's 'Chowt'-faced Rock was out of Bowman's Stuff and, if this is true, one can understand why Barker would be more than happy to bring this blood into his own terrier strain which saw much service with, firstly, his Pennine pack at Ousby, and then, after the family had moved to the Ullswater district during the early 1920s, the Ullswater foxhounds, now hunted by Braithwaite Wilson.

What I find fascinating is the little known fact that fell terriers were sent to members of the Ilfracombe badger digging club and that this blood was used on their white-bodied terriers which were similar to both Jack Russell types and Fox terriers, though

Gary Middleton of Windermere, a man who was a close friend of the Barkers, both Fred and Anthony, believes that Fell terrier blood, or certainly types resembling Fell terriers, had already entered the bloodlines of these early Fox terrier, or Jack Russell, types, long before Barker sent coloured terriers to the West Country as outcross blood. The fact that Barker did not go to the Carlisle and District Otterhound kennels for outcross blood, and certainly some of the best looking and working fox terriers were produced at these kennels during the latter part of the 1800s and the early part of the 1900s, choosing these hard-bitten badger digging dogs instead, may well indicate that his strain was already saturated with bloodlines from this hunt kennels, though that can only be educated guesswork. Another point to consider is that the terriers belonging to this club may already have had fell blood running through their veins and Barker may well have wanted to bring that blood, and it was certainly extremely game blood (a fact that only a fool would question), back into his own strain.

Ghyll (*left*), a Patterdale with a massively powerful head. Bull terrier blood is obvious in such terriers.

The early Patterdale terrier, referring to Fell terriers bred in this area (though some of the older generation used this term for fell terriers generally, whether they were bred in the Patterdale district or not, the term gradually falling into disuse after the 1912 meeting at Keswick which saw the improved strains given the name of their native home) was a mixture of old type coloured working terrier of the same stamp as the Lowther Castle strain, Bedlington, Fox terrier, and unregistered Fox terriers which were early Jack Russell types, such as those which came to the Lakes to hunt with Fred Barker at the Pennine foxhounds and, a little later, the Ullswater foxhounds. Irish bred terriers also entered the mix, for the harsh Irish terrier coat was much in evidence, not only on many of the terriers bred in the Ullswater hunt country, but also throughout the Lakes, these Irish working terriers being brought to this country by farm workers and those fleeing hard times back in their native land. Indeed, the Irish style of hunting is much in evidence in Cumbria, though less so these days.

The Irish have a long history of hunting with dogs and almost any breed will do. Once the crops have been gathered in the farmers will often come together, usually meeting at a crossroads and bringing along their own team of dogs. Many keep beagles, but, to be truthful, collies and terriers also make up the pack. The idea is to hunt a hare, but almost any quarry will do. Rats, rabbits, foxes, all are hunted, though very few are caught. As one keen hunting Irishman put it, 'at the end of a day's hunting all we had were torn coats, wet and sore feet and tired dogs!'

Particularly during the nineteenth century and the first half of the twentieth, this system was a common form of hunting in the Lake District, despite the fact that official hunts covered more or less all of the ground. Farmers, miners, quarrymen, people from all different backgrounds, adopted this Irish style of hunting that had undoubtedly been introduced by Irish immigrants, especially after the great famine of the 1840s. They would meet, bringing all sorts of curs with them; hounds, terriers, collies, even mongrels, and all kinds of quarry was hunted, ranging from rats through to badgers (all references to badger digging are from a time when it was legal, and very often respectable, to do so). Foxes were taken too. In the hunt countries of the shires anyone killing a fox outside of the official hunt was asking for trouble, for foxes were preserved for sport, but in the Lakes Reynard has always been considered as vermin and so any efforts to protect livestock are welcomed. The fellpacks cannot get around all of their hunt country on a regular basis, hunting different districts each week and sometimes only killing a fox or two at each visit, and so other methods are necessary (having said this, these packs continue to do an excellent job of controlling and dispersing foxes).

The hunting of these bobbery packs did much to aid fox control in Cumberland and many of these unofficial hunts were very successful indeed. Badgers were dug with much enthusiasm, but very often they were moved out of sheep rearing country and released unharmed in areas where they were less troublesome. Despite what some say to the contrary, badgers do take lambs and they will raid a henhouse with as much enthusiasm as a fox, their strength and digging ability often helping them to get past wire and other obstacles designed to prevent the loss of chickens and ducks. Middleton has lost hens to badgers on a number of occasions, their tell-tale pad-marks giving them away as they trailed through the snow. Badgers are predators, and very efficient predators at that, so it is not surprising that they can cause serious livestock losses to shepherds and farmers.

The west coast of Cumbria has seen a large settlement of Irish immigrants and nowhere was the Irish hunting system more in evidence than in this part of the Lakes. And nowhere else has the Irish terrier had more impact on fell terrier bloodlines, helping to shape the new improved strains of Lakeland terrier which gained Kennel Club recognition in 1921. The Irish terrier has helped shape other breeds too, but its impact was huge on the early fell terrier scene, though not just along the west coast, for, as I have already stated, early Patterdale terriers showed the influence of this Celtic breed of working terrier too; a breed that was incredibly versatile, being able to retrieve shot game and herd livestock, as well as hunting above ground and working below.

Roger Westmoreland, after saying that a large Irish population settling in Cumbria brought terriers with them and that these obviously entered local terrier strains, stated that, at one time half the terriers in the Patterdale district, even throughout the Ullswater country, were part spaniel, the terrier, 'Chowt'-faced Rock, having mated a spaniel (without the owner's consent I might add) and the pups, surprisingly, were absorbed into local terrier bloodlines (which says something about the gameness of this, one of the most famous fell terriers of all time, and the strain being bred by Fred Barker, firstly at Ousby, and then, after 1923, at Patterdale) and many chocolate puppies began to emerge after

Two chocolates and a black Patterdale (Dilly and JC). The chocolate colouring was undoubtedly introduced through Bedlington terrier influence.

this mating had occurred. The pups were no worse off for their gundog ancestry, however, for they proved extremely game and local hunters had no reservations about bringing this blood into their own strains, for no doubt this accidental mating had produced superb nose in the resultant offspring and their descendants; the great finding ability of the spaniel blood no doubt aiding these crossbred terriers when it came to finding in the huge borrans of the Lake District. Finding, it has to be remembered, is one of the most important qualities desired in a terrier that works with a fellpack.

This chocolate colouring was already showing in many fell strains, for some of the old time Bedlington terriers, considered the best and gamest workers in the world, were of a chocolate colouring, but this became much more common after the accidental mating between Barker's Rock and the spaniel. In fact, for chocolate coloured puppies to become so fixed in the original Patterdale terrier bloodlines 'Chowt'-faced Rock must have also carried the genes which produced this colouring, undoubtedly inherited from a Bedlington influence somewhere in his ancestry.

Because of the large-scale use of Fox terrier blood, including the unregistered types bred by southern badger digging clubs, many white-bodied terriers also appeared in Fell terrier litters. Plummer, in *The Fell Terrier*, mentions that many of these found a ready market among rabbit hunters who believed that they made superior rabbiters to the fell coloured puppies, and, while this is true (in my own district of Lancashire this view was often held by the older generation of countrymen who would say that Russell types were far better ratters and rabbiters, while fell types, usually called Border-Lakelands, were superior fox hunting dogs). It is also true to say that many of these white-bodied terriers saw service at hunt kennels throughout the Lakes and acquitted themselves very well indeed.

Johnny Richardson produced many white terriers in his litters of fells which were descended from the dogs of Jim Dalton, one of the greatest terrier breeders of all time, and these worked just as well for the Blencathra foxhounds. Barry Todhunter, the current Huntsman of this famous pack, has continued the line that Johnny bred and most of the Blencathra terriers are now white-bodied, though they do have a dash of Eddie Chapman Jack Russell running through their veins. Chapman breeds extremely game, sensible workers of a disposition that has been found in Devon for centuries, terriers that work their fox hard, but without causing undue damage to either the fox, or themselves. Todhunter requires a terrier to bay at its fox and persuade it to bolt, even after being hard-pressed by hounds, and this blood from Chapman's famous Foxwarren lines would help to produce terriers of such abilities. True, when hunting a lamb-worrying fox, or one that has slaughtered a farmer's chickens, or ducks, the culprit must be dealt with and a hard terrier, one that will close with its quarry and slay it underground, is required in this situation. Most fellpack Huntsmen will own, or know of someone who owns, such terriers, but in the main a more sensible terrier that will stand back and bay is desireable.

White-bodied terriers also became fairly common around the Patterdale district (Dalton's terriers had quite an impact in the Ullswater country, as did the Ilfracombe badger digging club Russell types, as well as Fox terriers bred and worked at the Carlisle and District Otterhound kennels, terriers bred down from the dogs of John Russell himself), but this colouring was bred away from as much as possible, for reds and black and tans were more highly favoured. Blacks were very rare in the Ullswater country, but not unknown, for Bedlington influence undoubtedly introduced this colouring into early Fell strains.

The history of the Bedlington terrier is shrouded in mystery to say the least. The Dandie Dinmont and the Bedlington obviously share the same common ancestry and I believe that a rough and ready terrier, similar no doubt to early untypey Fell terriers such as those found at Lowther Castle as early as the eighteenth century, was the rootstock of both of these famous breeds. Low-slung hounds similar in type to Dachshunds are what went into the mix producing the Dandie, while hardy rag Whippet and Bull terrier blood went into producing the Bedlington. That the Bedlington had a disposition which made them useful for dog-fighting is, I believe, proof enough that Bull terrier has entered the mix, though a very long time ago. The rag Whippets that were used to give enough leg-length so as to make them useful for rabbiting, were hardy tykes, small in stature, but as tough as old boots, able to take foxes with as much venom as a terrier (Whippets may, in part, be descended from ancient terriers). Fell terriers which show Bedlington influence are invariably up on the

Robinson *(far left)*, ex-huntsman of the original Wensleydale harriers and Frank Buck *(far right)* overseeing a dig on the Yorkshire moors. Is the terrier at the top simply a Jack Russell, or a terrier showing the influence of that brindle and white Bull terrier? Also note the black terrier which displays much Bedlington influence.

leg and have longer muzzles than their counterparts; undoubtedly from Whippet blood probably introduced during the nineteenth century, though possibly long before then.

The early Patterdale terrier displayed much Bedlington about it and these rough and ready tykes were used with the Patterdale hounds, which later became the Ullswater. I believe that this was when the term Patterdale terrier first began to be used, for terriers were often given the name of the pack they worked with.

Anthony Barker's famous Rock (a terrier also known as 'Chowt'-faced Rock, which can complicate the unravelling of bloodlines somewhat) was descended from Arthur Irving's

A typey terrier bred by Gary Middleton. The jacket, head and general type are exactly the same as those produced by Sid Wilkinson in Rock and Nettle in particular, the ancestors of all of Gary's dogs.

famous terrier, Robin, a superb looker and worker which Middleton believes was a mixture of Fell, Fox and Bedlington terrier, and which played an incredibly important part in the creation of the modern pedigree Lakeland terrier, as well as the terriers being bred at Patterdale by the Barkers, and at Glenridding by Sid Wilkinson. The Wilkinsons and the Barkers must be considered as *the* most important breeders of the original Patterdale terrier. In fact, they are amongst the top Fell terrier breeders the Lakes has ever produced, for very few Fell terriers are not descended from the dogs of these two very important hunting families.

Barker's Rock, an incredible worker and quite a typey dog, produced Sid Wilkinson's near-perfect terrier, Rock, a beautiful animal which stamped his type into his progeny and produced, not only very typey offspring, but also very game workers. Rock was Middleton's ideal terrier. For one thing, he was bred out of Anthony Barker's Rock, a terrier that is ranked as one of the best workers ever to have served with a fellpack and a dog which finished foxes quickly and efficiently. Like some of the terriers that served with Bowman, Rock also had the distinction of killing up to three foxes in one day's hunting; an incredible feat and one appreciated by any terrierman who has had his dog down to one tough hill fox, let alone three. Secondly, Sid Wilk's Rock was, like his sire, incredibly game and more than capable of finishing any fox that refused to bolt. Gary mentioned that Sid would often be out digging in the morning with Rock and then he would show him in the afternoon (in the Lakes, some hunts are followed by social events such as stick and terrier shows). He dug few badger using this terrier however, for he was just too hard for this quarry. Wilkinson took many foxes with this dog, though, and Gary, who was a close friend of the Barkers and the Wilkinsons, dug to this terrier on several occasions. The fact that Gary has bred the line Rock produced for over forty years tells the reader something of the abilities of this working terrier.

But it wasn't just the working abilities of this terrier that appealed to Gary. Middleton kept terriers from his grandfather's strain that had been bred around Dent for a few generations. Although they were game, they could not hold a candle to the terriers being produced by the Barkers and the Wilkinsons, either in looks, or working ability, so Gary took his bitches directly to Rock and sons of Rock. The offspring of these matings were not only vastly improved in the looks department, but were also superior workers to the strain Gary had first taken up as a young lad.

Hardasty's famous terrier, Turk, was around at the same time and I asked Gary why he hadn't based his lines on this terrier which, legend has it, was a far superior looker to Wilkinson's Rock. This simply isn't true. Gary stated that three terriers were the top winners at shows in the Lakes at that time and that all three shared the prizes. Some judges would put up Hardasty's Turk ahead of Rock, while others would put up Rock ahead of Turk, and, occasionally, Breay's bitch Skiffle would beat them both. Gary chose Rock ahead of Turk simply because Rock was a gamer, stronger animal with a much better head than Turk. He considered Wilk's Rock to be a little too broad in the chest, but other than that he was perfect. Turk was a superb worker and served Hardasty well at the Melbreak foxhounds, but Rock was a much harder, gamer dog. But it wasn't just for these reasons that Gary did not use Turk to start his own strain.

Though Gary (and many others) attempted to get to the bottom of Turk's breeding, he found it impossible to do so. Sid Hardasty may well have bred this terrier (see *The Fell Terrier*,) but Gary, who did the same show rounds as both Turk and Rock at the time, is adamant that a lot of mystery surrounded the breeding of this terrier and one of the rumours going around at the time was that Turk was found as a stray on the streets of Cockermouth and that he was given to Hardasty for use at the Melbreak. A terrier of uncertain ancestry was no good to Middleton who is a careful breeder who will only tolerate the very gamest stock, and the gamest stock at that time was that being bred by the Barkers and the Wilkinsons; stock whose ancestry could be traced right back to those terriers which served at the Pennine foxhounds at Ousby with Fred Barker.

Wilkinson's Rock was of such worth that almost all of the terriers to be found throughout the Ullswater country were bred out of him, so Gary had few problems in finding enough stud dogs to establish his own strain. He used Rock himself, other sons of Anthony Barker's Rock and, of course, sons of Wilk's Rock. Gary bred Mac by taking one of his bitches to Wilkinson's Rock. This terrier, like his sire and grandsire, and countless other terriers before them, was incredibly game.

Middleton was out with Anthony Barker and one or two other terrier lads as they hunted around Lake Ullswater. They came across a one-holed earth close to the shore and a terrier was entered. A badger proved to be at home and the terrier was soon evicted from the earth by the charging brock. Another terrier was tried and the same thing happened. Disgusted, Barker turned to Gary and asked him to try Mac who was by now doing cartwheels on the end of his lead. The terrier entered carefully however, and was soon hard at his quarry, standing his ground while Middleton dug towards him, despite Billy attempting to charge him out of the earth. Gary soon dug to a huge, unmoveable rock and knew that he could go no further. Amazingly, Mac seized his badger and was soon backing out of the earth, drawing his quarry from under that rock.

Gary soon tailed the badger and placed it in a sack for release out of sheep-rearing country (badgers were considered as vermin at the time and many farmers asked for them to be removed from their land), but he soon noticed that his terrier had been seriously injured. Mac's jaw had been badly broken. Turning to

Wes Swallow with Brock, a terrier bought from Frank Buck during the early eighties.

Mac, Barker stated 'he's a fair bit 'o' clowt', and the young Middleton knew that he was honoured to have such a compliment paid, for Barker had seen it all before, yet this dog still impressed him greatly. Barker also stated that the dog would probably be dead by the time Gary reached home, so they headed for Noran Bank, the Barker farmstead, and treated the dog there. Anthony's wife helped out and a sort of support was rigged up around Mac's jaw (veterinary treatment for small animals was still very much in the background at the time and so most treated their own) and, sure enough, his injuries healed well, though he did lose part of his jaw in the process. It was game qualities such as these that Middleton treasured and he set about 'locking in' those qualities very early on.

By breeding to Rock's line repeatedly, Middleton succeeded in locking in those fine qualities which have made his strain famous, both for their looks, and especially for their working abilities. Terriers which can win well at shows and perform out in the hunting field are what Gary has always aimed for, continuing to do so over forty years later. He stated that his dogs are fox killers, rather than bolters, and that the bitches are bred to bay and bolt foxes. This is the traditional standard for fell terriers, but there are exceptions to these rules. As with any strain, some of Middleton's dogs are not hard fox killers, but bayers. Nevertheless, they are still terrific workers. Likewise, some of his bitches will kill foxes, rather than stand off and bay, but generally his dogs are hard, while his bitches will stand back and bay.

Rex was one of the best terriers Middleton ever bred and, like Wilk's Rock, Gary bred from him frequently in order to lock in those precious qualities. Rex was bred out of Rock, a son of Wilk's dog, and Judy, a bitch bred out of a black and tan dog which belonged to the landlord of a pub at Dockray, and was another son of the inevitable Sid Wilikinson's Rock, and a bitch belonging to John Allen, also from Wilkinson's breeding. Rex carried several lines back to the Barker and Wilkinson strains and his looks and abilities well demonstrated this.

Although Middleton did much digging with this terrier, on both foxes and badgers, he was also loaned out to Dave Roberts, the legendary digging man from Manchester whose terriers were a mixture of Middleton blood and black stuff, and Ken Gould. Roberts dug with white-bodied terriers until he met Middleton who showed him a real working Lakeland doing its stuff. From then on Roberts switched to fell terriers and his dogs were incredibly game. Dave's famous worker, Rip, was out of Middleton stuff (Barry Wild says this is more than likely, but there are some doubts about this). This terrier is the ancestor of my own dog, Fell.

One of the most famous digs involving Rex, a terrier with which Gary won at the Great Yorkshire show, was in the company of Ken Gould. Rex was no baying terrier and he entered and got stuck into his fox very quickly indeed. Gary stated that he killed foxes almost casually, with seemingly little effort, and on more than one occasion he finished foxes without receiving a single bite. Some may find this difficult to believe, but my own dog, Ghyll, a descendant of Rex, on three separate occasions, killed foxes without receiving a bite from his opponent. By seizing a fox by the throat and throttling it, a terrier can avoid being bitten, though few are clever enough to achieve this.

Gould entered Rex and had to dig to the furious bumpings going on underground. After quite a bit of effort, Ken uncovered a dead fox, but Rex had gone further inside, the bumping sounds signalling that another fox was at home. Upon reaching his second dead fox, Rex was nowhere to be seen, but the telltale bumping began once more as a third fox was found. Gould dug onto fox number three and soon came upon Rex and yet another dead fox. It sounds like a tale from one of Bowman's hunts, but this was typical of the Barker and Wilkinson strain, for many terriers were bred which were capable of such incredible feats.

Middleton must have captured something very special in Rex though, for he mentioned how this terrier, a terrier which, after Wilk's Rock, was *the* most important stud in the strain, was able to boss even badgers in a way that Gary had never seen before, or has seen since. Rex was so aggressive and had such a commanding presence that few badgers would face him. Rex was also a superb seizure dog at the end of a dig, grabbing his quarry and pulling it out of the stop-end. Gary was a passionate foxhunter and badger digger during his younger years and terriers of such abilities were treasured by Middleton, and other fell-hunters such as Anthony Barker and Sid Wilkinson.

Middleton was out digging badgers one New Year's Day and decided to record his efforts for just that year, from one New Year's Day to the next. Along with scores of foxes, Gary dug 137 badgers that year, his digging partners varying from Brian Fleming to Anthony Barker. He said that, despite the fact that he had about twenty-five terriers in kennel at the time, with around twenty being entered terriers, he still found himself short on occasion, he had that much work on. He also dug with Cyril Breay on numerous occasions around Kirkby Lonsdale and the south Lakes. Dave Harcombe also travelled up to the Lakes and enjoyed a dig with Gary in the Winster valley. I have seen the photographs of this dig and a bitch named Trixie did most of the work on that occasion. Middleton's dogs are generally too hard for badger digging and so, when it was legal to do so, Gary often used his bitches. Even these though, could work a little too close to their quarry for comfort and digs to Lakeland bitches were often hair-raising experiences. Trixie was bred out of a dog named Chip who won everything, but again, he was first and foremost a worker and he produced first and foremost workers.

Punch was another grand terrier, a black and tan dog which won the first ever Lunesdale foxhounds terrier show, judged by Arthur Irving whose terrier, Robin, was responsible for 'polishing up' many strains, including Barker's and Wilkinson's, of both registered and unregistered Lakeland terriers. Robin was a wonderful worker and his refined type was responsible for producing terriers of a very smart appearance, but, again, they were first and foremost workers. Punch, though entered by Gary, was sent down Wales where he served with a footpack, eventually dying of what Middleton described as 'too much work'.

One of Buck's terriers with hounds from the re-formed Wensleydale harriers.

Jet was another grand looking and working terrier. The North Lonsdale had him on loan from Gary and he was lethal to any fox that refused to bolt. He killed far more than he bolted and eventually died of infected fox bites after the then Huntsman had failed to treat him properly. Middleton was livid and went to fetch his neglected terrier, but he had been left too long and he later died at Middleton's home.

Rex was put to a bitch, Floss, another coloured terrier, and this union produced Flint and Gravel, two white Lakelands which became very well known and which founded a dynasty of more typical Russell types than even the Russells themselves. Flint was purchased by Ken Gould and went on to become the cornerstone for Gould's Russell terriers which have a reputation as both lookers and workers throughout the country. Gravel, on the other hand, produced Billy, one of Middleton's most famous white Lakelands who was an incredibly good looking dog, very close to the standard of fourteen inch, fourteen pound Russell type in fact, who was also an outstanding worker. Gary retired him after five seasons because Billy was so hard that he had lost most of his teeth by this time. Billy retired and was used at stud in the south of England. This terrier, more than any other, is responsible for putting the correct type back into the Jack Russell terrier. In fact, the majority of registered Parson Russell terriers are descended from this dog. And no wonder, for Billy was of a type favoured by the Parson himself and is an almost exact replica of the dogs John Russell used with his pack of foxhounds. Middleton has photographs of early Russell types which undoubtedly gave rise to Fox terriers as well as Jack Russells, and they are identical to the stuff produced by the Middleton strain of Lakeland which, don't forget, carries many lines back to early Fox terriers. Lill Foiler, that Fox terrier bred out of Russell's Tip which served at the Carlisle kennels and produced top lookers and workers, is undoubtedly one of the ancestors of Middleton's strain, as are those two white terriers from the Ilfracombe badger digging club whose terriers were reputedly descended from those of Heinemann; terriers bred out of the original strain belonging to Russell himself.

Top Russell breeders have also visited Middleton's kennels in order to use even his coloured terriers to improve coat, type and head in their exhibits. The white Lakelands are outstanding looking animals which have all sprung from coloured parents and so, as long as there is Russell to Russell breeding, no coloured puppies should result, so using typical Lakeland coloured studs remains a very effective way of improving type in Jack Russell terriers. True, some breeders have stuck to traditional Russell types for their breeding programmes, but the type that is nearest to the standard favoured by the Parson himself is usually achieved with the use of Lakeland terrier blood, and the Lakelands bred by Gary Middleton in particular. Gary has no problems with showing white Lakelands in Russell classes for, as he stated, these are actually descended from the original stock that gave rise to Russells and Fox terriers in the first place.

Middleton considers his strain of terrier to be the true Patterdale, as he has simply carried on the breeding programme of the Barkers and the Wilkinsons, his stock being descended from that which was native to the Patterdale district. When Breay turned up with his smooth coated Bull type terriers at the Patterdale show, this type of working terrier was unknown and so Gary believes that the term is totally inaccurate when describing the terriers originally bred by Breay and Buck. Westmoreland believes this also. However, the truth is that this term is so widely used nowadays that, when Patterdale terriers are mentioned, one immediately thinks of the smooth coated black and red Bull terrier type earth dogs, which are now growing in popularity. Middleton's strain may be native to Patterdale, but these remain simply unregistered Lakeland terriers, not Patterdales, at least in the public's view anyway. Middleton's stock continues to work well today and they are used throughout the length and breadth of the country. A recent dig well illustrates how game this strain of terrier is, after Middleton has succeeded in locking in those vital qualities that have made them famous.

Gary had been losing livestock to thieving foxes and so, after a heavy fall of snow, he set out in search of the culprits. Having tracked two foxes up hill and down dale, the tracks finally led into a stone drain, or culvert, only a couple of fields away from his home. He entered Daz and waited outside the earth with his lurcher. No fox bolted and no sound came from below, so Gary, after quite a while of waiting, began digging holes throughout the length of this earth in order to locate his terrier. Three days later and with the help of friends from Yorkshire, Middleton finally found Daz who had killed one fox and was now attempting to get to another which was inside a very narrow offshoot of the main drain. Gary stated that the terrier was in no way trapped and that he had stayed there trying to reach his fox for those three days.

Staying qualities are considered vital in a working terrier and they do not come much better than this. The second fox was finally bolted and was taken by Gary's lurcher. After killing one fox, a feat in itself, Daz had stayed in a frozen drain for three days, undoubtedly because his fox was just a couple of feet away. These are just some of the reasons why Middleton continues to breed this strain which consistently throws up extraordinary working terriers of the highest order.

Only recently, another of Middleton's terriers bolted seven foxes from a drainpipe near Bradford. One was caught in the net, but the rest bolted and escaped. I have known there to be as many as five foxes in the same earth, but I have never heard of seven before. I have owned Middleton bred terriers and I have seen several others at work. Believe me, they are very much a working terrier today, despite the fact that he has been accused of producing show dogs only. Middleton estimates that if seventy-five per cent of your strain works, then you are doing really well. There are always going to be failures in any strain, but if the majority work, then you are onto a winner. I would say that at one time as much as ninety-five per cent of this strain would work, but in the last twenty years in particular many have taken up Middleton's strain for show purposes only and the working ability will always suffer under such circumstances. Although Middleton continues to enter and work his terriers, many do not. Working instinct will suffer when the working side is ignored and people breed for looks alone. But still, as working terriers, this strain, descended from the original Patterdale terrier, takes some beating.

3

ORIGINS OF MODERN
PATTERDALES

That Bull terrier blood has always played an important part in the development and uses of modern terrier breeds is, I believe, indisputable, and this is certainly very true in the case of the Patterdale terrier. The influence of Bull terrier blood is obvious to any who have even a slight knowledge of dog breeding, even though both Frank Buck and Cyril Breay, the originators, together with a colourful band of breeders and workers of terriers, of what is now known as the Patterdale terrier, both denied that they had used Bull terrier blood. Whether or not Bull terrier blood was introduced into these strains deliberately, or whether fell type terriers with Bull terrier in their make-up were used, will no doubt be debated for years to come, but one thing is absolutely certain – Bull terrier has had quite a lot of influence in the breeding of modern Patterdale terriers.

There is a long list of working terriers which show obvious Bull terrier influence. Early Fox terriers, for instance, often had very strong heads with short, powerful jaws. The Glen of Imaal also shows Bull terrier influence and is famous for its steel-trap jaws and great power which made them useful in the Irish trials for drawing badgers. Anyone who goes around working terrier shows today and examines the exhibits shown in Patterdale/black Fell/crossbred classes, will soon reach the conclusion that Bull terrier blood has indeed played an important part in the creation of this type of terrier, and it is easy to understand why when one looks into the background of this breed. The Patterdale, true, is a type of fell terrier, but has become so distinct from fell terriers that they must surely now be considered as a separate breed!

Cyril Breay was a fanatic of the quality of gameness. Middleton stated that he would have made a superb trainer for boxers, or

61

Midddleton's Ben, owned by Brian Fleming, and an incredible worker. My dog, Fell, is descended from this terrier.

some other sport which required extraordinary gameness and endurance to be a participant. Instead, Breay entered the world of working terriers and, as Roger Westmoreland said, bred only the gamest of dogs to the gamest of bitches. The gamest of terriers at that time were those which had a history connected with Bull terriers. Breay started out in Sealyham terriers during the early part of the twentieth century and it is said that this breed originated, in part, from the now extinct Cheshire white terrier, a small, agile Bull terrier which was as game as they come. Fox terrier was added to the mix during the latter part of the nine-teenth century, and thus the breed carried quite a few lines back to Bull terriers, making them extremely game and useful during a golden age for pedigree terriers when they were still small and agile enough to be useful working breeds.

I recently came across a picture painted by Ben Marshall at the beginning of the nineteenth century. The subject was Francis Dukinfield and his pack of harriers, but what fascinated me most was a small, all-white terrier which showed obvious Bull terrier influence, no doubt being a cross 'twixt a Cheshire terrier and one of the rough and ready white bodied terriers that later gave rise to both the Jack Russell and the Fox terrier. Dukinfield hunted the hills east of Manchester, some of which is now Pennine foxhounds country, but no doubt his foxes took him down onto the great plain of Manchester, and this country is difficult indeed.

Nuttall Patterdale Terriers. Earth dogs of substance!

Many earths are undiggable and Dukinfield would have needed a terrier capable of finishing reluctant foxes below ground, hence the reason for earth dogs with Bull terrier in their lines. Marshall had a reputation for painting to a true likeness, so I have absolutely no doubts at all that this portrait is an accurate representation of the type of terrier being used at the time. Put a black jacket on that all-white terrier doing its best to keep up with Astley's harriers, and you have a modern smooth coated Patterdale terrier!

Breay soon turned to Fell terriers, possibly finding them the gamest stock around, and from then on discontinued breeding and working Sealyhams, though he did bring this strain into his fell terrier bloodlines, but quickly bred away from these white bodied types. This is just one area in which Bull terrier blood entered into the Buck/Breay breeding programme, through the influence of Sealyham terriers.

Buck's Tiger was one of the most important dams in the Buck/Breay breeding programme and her brindle colouring suggests that she had Bull terrier in her not too distant ancestry. Mated to a Bedale hunt terrier, a superb worker which had much Border blood in its make-up, she continued the line which would eventually lead to the type now referred to as a Patterdale terrier. Tiger was descended from the old type Sealyham which was created partly by using Cheshire terriers, and Border terriers were also created with the use of Bull terrier blood, the massively powerful heads testifying to this fact. Chris Rainford's Border terrier, Keeper, the grandsire of my own terrier of the same name, had one of the biggest heads I have ever seen on a terrier and he could finish a fox in seconds. If Bradley's Rip was indeed the ancestor of the Buck and Breay strain, possibly through the Bedale hunt terrier, then Bull terrier blood was rife in these early foundation terriers.

John Winch told Brian Plummer (see *The Sporting Terrier*) that the North-east of England was once famed for its agile fighting pit-Bull terriers, some of which were harsh coated. I believe that such terriers, when mixed with the blood of Irish, Fell and Bedlington type terriers, gave rise to the Border terrier. Borders have had quite an impact on the strain later to be called Patterdales and thus Bull terrier blood has entered the strain in this way, as well as through the early influence of Sealyhams. Also, the blue dog Tink, the sire of Tiger, was a fell terrier which was of obvious Bedlington ancestry and there can be no doubt that these tiny pit dogs were also used in the creation of Bedlingtons, for these were used for pit fights and were just as game, if not gamer, than any Bull terrier. Hence, the Buck/Breay breeding programme carried several lines back to Bull terriers.

Many claim that Bull terrier blood was introduced into this strain at some point and the type now known as Patterdales certainly show a great influence from this breed of fighting dog, though exactly how this type of terrier emerged is a mystery. Certainly, many of the terriers bred by Buck and Breay would pass for even first-cross fell/Bull terriers, but they strongly denied that they had used such a cross in their strain. There are four possible ways in which this type of terrier began to emerge during the late 1950s, but particularly throughout the 1960s:

(1) Because there are several lines carried back to Bull terrier blood through the influence of Sealyham, Border and

Bedlington blood, the type emerged and became fixed in the strain through inbreeding, a practice certainly employed by Breay in particular who was a well educated man and had a good working knowledge of genetics.

(2) Fell terriers carrying maybe half, or even a quarter Bull terrier blood were introduced into the strain at some point, and fell terriers were often crossed with Bull terriers, the smaller fighting dogs, in times past, in order to improve head and courage.

(3) Bull terrier blood was deliberately introduced in the late 1950s, or some time prior to this, when this type of terrier, smooth coated, muscular, Bull-headed types, began to emerge.

(4) The type is simply due to the influence of Border terrier blood introduced through descendants of Bradley's Rip and the Bedale hunt terrier.

I strongly believe that the fourth option should be totally discounted as the smooth coated terriers were too much Bull terrier in type for that influence to have come through Border terrier blood alone. Also, at the time that Border blood played a very important part in the Buck/Breay strain, the offspring produced were incredibly sane, sensible workers and were more Lakeland/Fell terrier in type. Many, it is true, could finish a fox that just would not bolt, but they were capable of doing so without receiving a mauling in the process. This you would expect from Border terrier influence.

During the sixties and seventies in particular, many of the smooth coated Bull-headed type terrier produced by both Buck and Breay, grew increasingly hard and took fearful punishment as a result. Those who dug with these terriers at the time state that many of these Bull type fell terriers would seize a fox anywhere and hang on for grim death. This was confirmed by the late Brian Plummer who dug with several Breay/Buck terriers during the sixties and seventies. Middleton said that he has seen Breay-bred terriers latch onto the leg of a fox refusing to let go even though the fox was free to inflinct severe damage on its opponent. This disposition rules out the type originating from Border terrier influence and indicates instead that Bull terrier blood was responsible for such lack of sense underground. That leaves us with the other three options.

Frank Buck (*right*)with a terrier which has obviously been tidied up with Lakeland blood. The man next to Frank was the terrierman for the Zetland hunt and Frank got quite a few almost pure Borders from this man. Note the almost pure Border he is showing.

Option one, for me, is out of the question, for there is just too much Bull terrier about the strain for it to have sprung up through genetics. I firmly believe that options two and three are the most likely source of these Bull type terriers now known as Patterdales. Breay was fanatical about gameness and for him the joy of hunting was in the courage and endurance shown by the terriers he worked. Many may disagree, but this is surely one good reason why Breay would introduce Bull terrier blood, either by using a Bull terrier stud, or a Fell terrier which was maybe half, or a quarter bred Bull terrier. But is there any evidence to suggest that this is indeed a possibility?

My research has led to a black terrier owned by a postmistress at a small village near Garsdale, the home of the late Josie Akerigg who shared in the Buck/Breay breeding programme. This terrier was of breeding unknown, but was obviously a Fell type, and was used, it is said, to produce many of the black terriers this strain became famous for. This terrier was obviously very game, for neither Breay, nor Buck, would use non-workers. It is just possible that this unknown black terrier was partly Bull terrier bred and put into the strain those qualities that betray this ancestry to some degree. I questioned Roger Westmoreland about this black terrier and he has no recollections of such a dog. Westmoreland dug with both Breay and Buck from the late fifties onwards and also kept and bred this strain. Still, it is possible that such a terrier existed and was used without it becoming common knowledge. If option two is indeed the way in which the Bull headed smooths began cropping up in this strain, then this black terrier may well have been responsible for this.

The first black terrier to appear in the strain was in 1936 and this was bred by Cyril Breay who gave the terrier to Buck, for Breay wasn't too keen on blacks and gave most of them away, or sold them to keen badger diggers and foxhunters. However, as Westmoreland told me, there were black terriers around long before then, no doubt this colour being introduced to Fell types through Bedlington influence, but these were not the smooth, Bull headed type of terrier which began to emerge in the Buck/Breay strain during the late fifties and on through the sixties and seventies.

Option three, though very controversial, cannot be ruled out. I have it on good authority that a Mr and Mrs Williams, who lived near Sedbergh, were close friends of Cyril Breay and they would often participate in organised badger digs together. The Williams bred a very game strain of Border terrier which were used on these digs and performed very well indeed. This was at a time when Badger digging was both legal and considered respectable and most terriermen would engage in this sport; even some, like the Williams family, who bred Kennel Club stock. My source was a good friend of Mrs Williams and spent many a happy afternoon being plied with whisky in her sitting room. Mrs Williams told my source that Cyril Breay began bringing Frank Buck along on some of these organised badger digs and that Buck brought with him a pied Bull terrier, which he used as a seizure dog at the end of digs.

Middleton's Jack, one of the early terriers of his strain and a wonderful worker, considered to be the true Patterdale type.

She also related how this Bull terrier was just as keen to latch onto her Border terriers, as it was the badgers themselves, and how, in the end, she was forced to ask Mr Breay not to bring Buck along anymore, if he was going to bring that Bull terrier, which she described as an absolute nuisance, along with him. Could it be that Buck and Breay were testing that Bull terrier as to gameness with a view to bringing it into their own strain of working terrier?

Roger Westmoreland stated that he never knew of Buck ever owning a Bull terrier and none of the farmers they dug vermin for ever mentioned such a dog. He also said that Buck was very much against the addition of Bull terrier blood to any strain of working terrier. I find this a little odd, however, for the bottomless courage of any strain of working terrier has come about because of Bull terrier blood. Wendy Pinkney, now 'terrierman' for the Golden Valley foxhounds where her husband, Will, is the current Huntsman, confirmed that Buck was very much against the addition of either Bull terrier, or pedigree Lakeland terrier blood being added to a Fell strain. I also questioned Max Buck, Frank's son who now works his terriers with the West of Yore, just one of the packs his father hunted with, and he has no recollection of any Bull terriers at the Buck household, further stating that his father was very much against the addition of Bull blood. So it seems very unlikely, on the surface, that Buck and Breay ever used Bull terrier blood deliberately to improve courage in their strain.

However, first of all my source is absolutely reliable, having been told of this by an eyewitness, one of the organisers of these badger digs in fact. Secondly, because Buck was so much against the use of Bull blood does not rule out the possibility that it was indeed used. Buck was strongly against the use of pedigree Lakeland blood, but only after he had used such blood to bring into his strain and he had seen the bad results from such an outcross. It is just possible that Buck and Breay did indeed use this pied Bull terrier, after testing it to the full, to improve courage, head and strength of jaw in their earth dogs, for this strain did have severe faults with bad mouths and bone at times, an inevitable consequence of establishing a strain through inbreeding, a practice used by both Buck and Breay (Frank Buck once told Wendy Pinkney never to put son to mother, but father to daughter, or nephew to aunt was okay).

I have absolutely no doubts at all that Frank Buck did indeed turn up at those organised digs with a pied Bull terrier. Whether he owned it, or simply borrowed it is impossible to say, but one thing is certain, he did use a Bull terrier at the end of those digs. Frank usually shot any foxes and badgers he dug, Westmoreland stating that Frank treated his quarry in a very humane manner, always killing them quickly at the end of a dig in what is now considered to be the most humane way of all, with a single shot to the head. However, these organised badger digs often resulted in the captive quarry being taken alive and unharmed and then later released well away from sheep-rearing country, if the farmer so wished. Hence the reason why a seizure dog was used, although, to be quite frank, most game terriers did hold a badger at the end of a dig, without Bull terriers being used, though many did resort to such tactics and the agile fighting Bull terriers of Northern England were often used as seizure dogs by sporting miners when digging badgers. I think it most likely that this Bull terrier belonged to a friend, or an aquaintance of Buck, and was being tested as to gameness.

Could it be that Buck was so against the use of Bull blood being added to a strain of working terrier because, as in the case of the pedigree Lakeland, he had experienced the results of such actions first hand? Could it be that the Bull cross produced a 'won't give an inch' sort of disposition which meant that much sense was lost underground in the resultant offspring, producing terriers which closed with their quarry, grabbing them anywhere and taking fearful maulings as a consequence? Buck preferred bolting terriers when out with hounds, for he acted as terrierman for several packs over the years, but he also did much hunting for local farmers and even ran his own hounds at times. Wensleydale is full of bad earths and a terrier which closed with and finished a reluctant fox in such places, usually undiggable spots, would no doubt be of much use to Buck. Bull terrier blood would achieve such characteristics!

If Bull blood was indeed introduced to this strain, as, I believe, it undoubtedly was through either option two, or option three, then I am sure this was done to correct faults in the strain, as well as to spice up courage. Bull blood does make the offspring mute in many cases, making digging to them almost impossible before locators arrived on the scene, and it also made terriers too hard. As I stated earlier, many Breay bred terriers, although having a reputation as fearless workers, closed with their quarry, grabbed it anywhere and hung on while the fox retaliated and inflicted severe wounds on its opponent. No matter what those say who are adamant that Bull blood was never used, this characteristic betrays the fact that it was. True, Bull blood has been added since the death of Breay and even more Bull terrier like offspring have resulted, but before this occurred many of the terriers bred by both Breay and Buck, had more than a hint of Bull about them.

My money would be on a Bull terrier cross being used early on and the type refined, especially by Breay who had a good working knowledge of genetics and who was capable of producing much more refined, typey terriers than either Buck, or any other of the colourful band who bred and worked these terriers. By the late fifties, the terriers emerging were typey indeed and Breay won many shows, even beating Wilk's Rock, in my opinion the most perfect terrier to come out of the Lakes, and Hardasty's Turk, on occasion. Breay and Buck's terriers were smooth, Bull headed types, which, as Middleton stated, were very typey indeed, but not all were of this type. Some were traditional Fell types, but most had the large, powerful head associated with this strain, being rough coated. Not all were black and red either, for some were black and tan. Bingo was a very rich red in colour, more akin to a ripe conker just out of its spiky shell. This colour is still seen on many Bull headed smooth Breay type terriers at shows today and this colour is more associated with Bull terriers than it is with Fell terriers!

When talking about the 'Buck and Breay strain', I suppose this is a little unfair. True, during the early years, Buck and Breay certainly created this strain together, with Breay's expertise meaning that typey terriers, as well as top class workers, were produced, but later on others added very much to the breeding programme of this strain of terrier. Good terriermen such as Roger Westmoreland, Ted Jenkinson of Chorley, Nev Chatwood, John Whaley of Mallerstang, Brian Nuttall, John Parkes and, of course, Josie Akerigg, all played an important part in the later

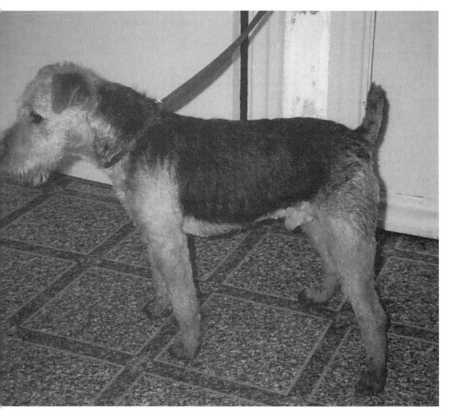

A black and tan out of Barry Wild's black stuff. This strain has been tidied up with Middleton blood.

breeding programme of this strain, particularly from the fifties onwards.

One of the most important later brood bitches was a terrier belonging to Josie Akerigg. Lasty (an unusual name, even by Fell terrier standards) was a three-quarter bred Border type Fell terrier which, Middleton believes, was bred out of the Williams' game strain of Border terrier that had proven itself so often on organised badger digs which both Breay and Buck attended. Brian Plummer, in his superb book, *The Sporting Terrier*, states, in the section on Borders, that Breay, after the Bedale hunt terrier had mated Tiger, never again used Border blood in the strains which gave rise to Patterdale terriers, but this simply isn't true, for this bitch, Lasty, was extensively used and bred many litters when mated to stud dogs such as Breay's famous dog, Bingo. Breay preferred smooth, or very hard coated red terriers and mainly smooths were produced in litters bred out of Lasty, though, as Westmoreland stated, she also produced hard coated offspring.

The main quality, however, that Breay and Buck sought in their terriers was gameness and only the very best dogs were put to the very best bitches. This says something of the quality of this bitch, Lasty, which bred much of the later stuff of Buck and Breay breeding. Middleton told me that Josie Akerigg had a real knack of catching foxes and that he took very large hauls, possibly even more than Buck and Breay, with his terriers, and so Lasty had much experience behind her before she began to be used as a brood bitch. It is a curious fact that some have a superior way with them when it comes to terrier work. A Newcastle lad known as Mac, another friend of Gary Middleton, also had a real knack of catching foxes and, like Akerigg, took large hauls with his terriers, most of which were from Middleton's strain. The terriers Gary sent up to the North-east saw much service at both fox and badger.

Bingo (Bing) was an extremely game terrier and he bred some extremely game offspring too. Rusty and Kipper are very well known, but one of the gamest of Bingo's sons, a lesser-known dog, was a smooth terrier called Ripple which was bred by Josie Akerigg, who must be considered as one of the most important breeders of this type of terrier during Buck and Breay's later years. Ripple served at the Lunesdale foxhounds after Nicholson had taken over from Walter Parkin as Huntsman. He killed far more foxes than he bolted and so was used on lamb-killing foxes during the spring months when hounds are frequently called out to deal with problem predators. As Middleton stated, this terrier quickly latched onto its fox and finished it below ground, thus it would not have suited many lowland packs, which require a terrier to stand back and bolt the quarry. Ripple was as hard as iron and was possibly gamer than even Bingo, his sire.

Roger Westmoreland, among others, still breeds Buck/Breay terriers and a few serve at the Consiston foxhound kennels. Westmoreland is quick to point out that these are not in any way like the muscular Bull terrier type Patterdales being bred today and are very much how Buck and Breay wanted their terriers to be, but the truth is that many Bull type terriers were produced by both of these famous terrier breeders. Kipper, Rusty, Bingo, Ripple, and scores of others, were Bull terrier in type, while others were more typical Fell terriers, displaying quite a bit of Border influence in their make-up.

When Mr Breay died during the 1970s, he left a kennel of typey red terriers, some smooth, others hard coated, but blacks were noticeable by their absence. Buck continued to breed and use typey black terriers, but these showed more Border influence than they did Bull terrier, so maybe Buck was unhappy with these types and deliberately bred away from them. No doubt this was because he was terrierman to the Bedale and West of Yore foxhounds and the Bull types which went in and slaughtered their fox quickly, were of little use to such packs who wished their foxes to be bolted unharmed. Terriers such as Ripple and Bingo were of virtually no use to a shire pack who wish to show sport for their riders, except, maybe, at springtime when lamb killing foxes must be dealt with severely.

Both Buck and Breay bred extremely game working terriers that were a mix of Sealyham, Border and Fell terrier blood, the Fell type terriers being the dominant force in the creation of these strains. Terriers such as Bingo, Rusty and Ripple betrayed the fact that Bull terrier blood had also entered this strain at some point and by some means. Of course, it can only be speculation when attempting to explain exactly how this occurred, and why, but I firmly believe that all of the evidence points to the fact that somehow Bull terrier blood entered the Buck/Breay breeding programme. Others have added Bull terrier to the strain later on, but I am certain that this course of action would not have met with approval from either Frank Buck, or Cyril Breay. The addition of Bull terrier blood can only succeed in taking even more sense away from these terriers. Some already show a Bull terrier disposition; going straight into their quarry, latching onto it and taking fearsome punishment as a result. One often comes across these terriers at shows and they bear many scars, which betray a lack of sense while underground. True, they are incredibly courageous, but very stupid at the same time. The traditional Fell terrier, and the Patterdale is a type of Fell terrier, should be courageous, yes, but it should also have enough sense not to get itself too badly knocked about. A terrier that has the task of killing a lamb-killing fox deep inside a huge borran must have the strength to get itself out of such an earth after its task is completed. A badly injured terrier may not succeed in doing so.

Some of the Buck/Breay bred terriers, particularly from the sixties onwards, were incredibly hard and many lacked sense enough to stay out of trouble. One of these was a large black, hard coated terrier called Rip. He had more than a hint of Bull terrier about him and he had been worked in the Lake District for a few seasons before finishing his days in Lancashire. Rip was incredibly hard and I worked with this terrier, who was born in the late seventies, on a number of occasions. One of the more memorable outings was one frosty morning in February during the early eighties.

To call it a frosty morning is rather an understatement, however, for the ground was as hard as iron, a dense white covering everywhere. It was so cold that, when I approached a dry stone drain I could actually feel the body heat of a fox coming out of the confined space of the earth. I didn't need the terriers to confirm what I already knew, but Pep, my Jack Russell, and Merle, my lurcher, soon did so. They were as keen as mustard and so Pep was soon released into the drain. A few seconds later she was baying strong and keen, the fox standing its ground and refusing to bolt.

We sat outside the earth, trembling with a mixture of excitement and extreme cold, silent in the hopes that Reynard would soon make a bid for the outside world, but it wasn't to be. Pep continued to bay steadily and the occasional raising of her voice meant that she was dodging the lunges of her quarry, while doing her best to keep the pressure on. My Fell terrier bitch, Rock, was just beginning her illustrious career at this time and she would go in and have a bay for a while, but it was Pep who did most of the work.

Eventually, once it became obvious that Reynard was not going

A youngster with a good head and jacket; bred by Middleton.

to shift, we began digging. I had only just left school at the time and was out of work, so I could not afford the luxury of a locator. Instead, I did all of my digging the old fashioned way; by ear. Unfortunately, I only had a grafter with me that day, one of the small folding type, and so it was hard going. Barry and I took turns trying to cut through that frost-hardened ground which had been penetrated for a good few inches, with the grafter giving out before the frost did. It snapped clean in half and so Barry headed off to a nearby farm for digging tools. I did a great deal of fox digging in those days (an injury to the elbow and a growing army of anti-hunting ramblers mean that digging in many areas is now nigh-on impossible for me, though I still enjoy a few good digs each season) and so my little grafter had seen some punishment, finally giving out on this testing ground. Not to worry, Barry was soon back with a pick and spade and progress, though still hard going, was much quicker than previously.

After a great deal of effort, we finally broke through, between two and three feet down. This is a very shallow dig, I know, but the frost-hardened first few inches eventually gave out to impacted stony clay, so the going was extremely difficult throughout. Once through to the drain, we removed the top flagstone and we were in at last. The trouble with working drains is that it is difficult to pinpoint exactly where the terrier is, for sound can be very misleading in such an earth. We discovered, to our dismay, that we had missed the mark by a good few feet. Pep was still baying and teasing at her fox, but she couldn't move it. Rock was only very young and inexperienced, so she was of little use just then. We had two options. Either start digging again, not a happy prospect after our experience of this ground, or Barry could go home and fetch Rip. The terrier belonged to a friend of his, but he could borrow the dog at any time. We decided to go with option two, for, though both of us loved digging and often took part in some gruelling digs, some of which had lasted for upwards of twelve hours, this ground was incredibly difficult to break through and so neither of us relished the thought of tackling such a dig yet again. Rip, it was hoped, would drive that fox to our break, where I could seize it and pull it out. Well, that was the theory anyway. We would have to wait and see if it worked.

Pep continued to bay steadily at her fox until Barry arrived, with Rip pulling eagerly at his lead, keen to latch onto the terriers, let alone the fox. After some effort, I managed to call Pep out of the earth and Rip replaced her. Bedlam broke out. With a Bull terrier-like disposition, Rip charged into the earth and did away with any preliminary baying, waiting his chance to seize his foe by the throat and throttle it. Instead, he seized his fox at the first chance he got and drove it back to where I was waiting. I tailed the fox and pulled it out of the earth, but quickly let go as it rounded on me, releasing its grip on the terrier. Merle was in the way however, receiving a bad bite to his leg. He yelped, but then erupted with rage and quickly killed his fox, shaking it as a terrier shakes a rat. Rip had certainly done what was required of him, but with little, or should I say, no sense, in the process, his muzzle looking like a piece of raw liver after he had seized the fox by the shoulder, allowing it to strike at him time and again; a common fault in many Buck/Breay terriers of the sixties and seventies. A disposition such as this betrays Bull terrier influence in the not too distant past.

Frank Buck at a spot from where he rescued a terrier. Buck
carried out many rescues from such places.

Whatever went into the mix, one thing is certain; Frank Buck
and Cyril Breay, together with a few other terrier breeders,
succeeded in producing an extremely game and courageous race
of working terrier. True, at times and in certain bloodlines,
terriers were produced with that Bull terrier-like disposition of
seizing foxes anywhere and taking terrific punishment as a consequence, but in the main this strain has proven itself both game
and sensible at all types of quarry. Although Breay was a keen

77

fox-hunting man, he was also a very keen badger digger (Middleton, who dug badger with Breay on several occasions, says that Mr Breay couldn't dig for toffee, but that he always had plenty of young helpers who would dig all day for him) and he dug many with his strain, proof enough that several sensible workers also sprang up in litters. Indeed, he was a keen participant in those organised badger digs with Mr and Mrs Williams. Frank Buck, however, much preferred digging and bolting foxes, though, as Roger Westmoreland stated, he also dug hundreds of badgers during those days when it was legal, and considered respectable, to do so. There was no political correctness in those days and so badger digging was popular, considered as an effective means of pest control, for badgers do take farm livestock. They are predators, so this should surprise no-one, not anyone with any common sense anyway!

A few words concerning badger digging are apt at this stage, for badger baiting, a totally different activity, is confused with the former and has been used by the anti brigade to discredit legitimate terrier work. In the days when badger digging was legal, farmers would often request terrier lads to come on to their land and dig the badgers out, very often asking that the occupants be released elsewhere, usually out of sheep country (badgers will prey on lambs and I suspect that many are taken by these creatures and foxes blamed, though, of course, foxes will also take lambs, and far more frequently than do badgers). If possible, they would be released into an unused sett, but still, if not, then the released badgers would soon find somewhere to settle, for they are incredible diggers and can have a sett dug out in no time.

Badgers, being part of the Mustelid family, are incredibly hardy creatures and are far tougher than any terrier. Usually, baying terriers, that is, those with a disposition to stand off their quarry and bark at it, nipping and teasing so as not to allow the badger to dig its way further on, were used. The loud baying would guide the diggers to where the badger was hiding in the dark passage. At the end of the dig, the terrier would rush in and seize the badger, thus holding it while the digger tailed it and put it in a sack. Badgers have very thick skin and dense fur, thus they are not harmed by a terrier grabbing hold of it, whilst it is secured for release elsewhere. Some farmers, however, would require the badger to be dispatched. In this situation a single shot to the head would kill it instantly. Badgers do not suffer when being dug. A baying terrier is merely an irritation to such creatures and one thing is for sure, badgers are not terrified of anything. Badger digging was a humane way of controlling these creatures and is as different to baiting as black and white, chalk and cheese.

Baiting involved pitting one, or very often several, dogs against a badger which, in some cases, had been injured, or had had its fangs extracted so that it could do little damage to the dogs set upon it. The badger usually expired of shock after enduring several hours of cruelty. When a badger was not injured, or had some of its teeth removed, severe injuries to the terriers usually resulted, until, that is, the badger had no fight left in it. No normal human could gain any pleasure from such horrendous activities and true countrymen condemn utterly such contemptible acts. But such acts must not be confused with badger digging which was a humane way of ridding farmers of troublesome tenants from their land. Cyril Breay and Frank Buck removed many badgers for farmers in Cumbria and Yorkshire and they did so with humanity, far removed from the degraded cruelty of badger baiters.

It has been said that Cyril Breay broke the rules when it came to the breeding of working terriers and in many ways this was true. For one thing, while other fell hunters were producing smaller terriers that were very narrow and very often between ten and twelve inches at the shoulder, Cyril Breay would breed very powerful terriers that would sometimes reach as much as sixteen inches at the shoulder. Of course, many levelled out at around thirteen inches, but, because of the muscular build of these earth dogs, they looked much bigger. Many of Breay's terriers may have taken a little longer to get to their fox, but get there they did. And, because of this power, they proved most useful both as fox and badger hunting dogs.

Badgers are incredibly difficult creatures for a terrier to handle. When a large badger charged at its foe, it needed a dog with some power behind it in order to hold the quarry until the diggers reached the spot. Especially in larger setts, this could be a most difficult task and a powerful, strong-willed dog was needed, one that would stand its ground and prevent 'Brock' from getting past and away to certain escape. Also, if a terrier did not work its badger hard, lying close to its quarry and keeping it occupied, then it could so easily dig on further and elude capture, becoming lost in an earth now full of confusing scent which none but the most experienced of dogs could fathom. Breay's terriers had the power and the courage to be most useful as badger digging dogs, though it is also true to say that many were just too hard for the task, especially some of his later stock which had a look of Bull terrier about them. A hard terrier would often attack its badger as eagerly as it would a fox and very serious injury, very often death, would be the result. If a hard terrier could not be reached quickly enough when at 'Brock', then the uncovering of a dead dog was usually the result.

The modern Patterdale terrier, although very much a product of the breeding programmes of quality terriermen such as Brian Nuttall and John Parkes, along with quite a few other dedicated breeders, has its origins in the breeding and working schemes of that colourful band which included such notables as Josie Akerigg and Roger Westmoreland, but most of all Cyril Breay and Frank Buck. Few terriers in Britain today do not have the blood of Buck and Breay's terriers in their pedigree. When asked by Wendy Pinkney how one of my bitches was bred, I replied that she was out of Breay and Buck's old stuff. 'Most of the terriers in Britain are out of Breay and Buck stuff' was her reply!

4

THE MODERN PATTERDALE

Although I believe that a certain amount of Bull terrier blood was responsible for the type of terrier which gave rise to Breay's famous Bingo, and others of similar type, I also believe that less careful breeders have added much more Bull terrier to the mix and I cannot for the life of me think why this should be so, for Buck/Breay bred terriers are amongst the very gamest in the world and further addition of such blood is totally unnecessary, not to mention damaging to the strain. Of course, Bull terrier blood has featured fairly heavily in the early days of most, if not all, terrier breeds, having been included in order to improve courage, strength and head, particularly jaw strength, in order that these earth dogs could give a good account of themselves against the fiercest of quarry. Not only creatures such as badgers and otters, but also wildcats, for these felines were once found throughout Britain and were frequently hunted with terriers. For a dog to walk into those incredibly sharp, and fast-striking, claws, a terrier would need guts to spare and it was Bull terrier blood that provided such courage. The trouble is, this cross usually produced stupidity too and fearsome punishment would be taken by the resultant offspring, though sense would very often return with later generations.

Sense is highly prized by terriermen who know of the damage a foolhardy terrier will receive whilst attempting to shift a fox from a good vantage point from where it can continually strike at its foe and cause untold damage to the face and jaw of its opponent. A sensible terrier will get bitten, true, but it will also quickly learn how to work its fox cleverly so that it dodges many of these lightning-fast strikes and avoids going jaw to jaw with its quarry; a certain way of getting very badly damaged. A terrier that gets bitten will heal in no time at all, but one that goes jaw to jaw and wrestles with its foe will be out of action for weeks afterwards. This is of little use to the man who has foxes to control on a regular basis, for his terriers must be available sometimes for as many as two or three days a week.

Although Breay and Buck bred several terriers which would literally seize their fox anywhere and receive severe punishment as a consequence, it is also true to say that they bred many sensible workers which were capable of killing a fox without getting too badly knocked about. Some of the modern Patterdale terriers which have obviously had Bull terrier added to the strain since the death of Breay, often have one thing in common; they are badly scarred and usually have pieces of jawbone missing. These are proudly paraded at shows and more ammunition is given to the growing number of opponents to terrier work.

As both Brian Nuttall and Gary Middleton have stated, Fell terriers, including Patterdales of course, are gamer than Bull terriers, but with much more sense, so what is the point of adding even more Bull terrier blood which has already ruined many once sensible strains? Not only does the addition of Bull terrier blood take away sense, but it also increases size greatly. I have seen

A terrier displaying those qualities 'locked in' from Wilkinson's famous Rock.

sixteen-inch terriers get to ground and reach their fox simply because they had narrow fronts and a spannable chest, but this addition can greatly increase chest size as well as leg-length and the resultant offspring cannot get anywhere but the largest of badger setts; places they are no longer allowed to enter. At one time such terriers would have been used as seizure dogs at the end of badger digs, but that is now illegal and dogs of this size are useless as working animals, so why breed them in the first place? Further addition of Bull terrier blood is most undesirable in Patterdale terriers and serves no useful purpose at all. Anyone who has worked with any modern Patterdale which is still bred along the old lines will agree with me when I say that they are already ultra-game and need the addition of Bull blood like they need a hole in the head!

Other terriers from the Buck/Breay strain have been infused with unregistered Lakeland terrier blood in order to improve chances at working terrier shows, but this has done little to harm the working qualities of these strains, for both Cowen and Middleton blood have played an important part in improving type in Patterdales and the stud dogs from these strains have been excellent workers. There is some controversy over the breeding of Ken Gould's famous terrier, Smithy. It is reputed that Cowen blood was responsible for the improved looks of this dog, when put with a Nuttall bred bitch, but at the time of Smithy's growing popularity as an incredible worker and stud dog, it was also rumoured that Middleton's incredibly good looking and working terrier, Rex, had sired this dog. Of course, it is now very likely impossible to prove the exact breeding of this, one of the most famous of all Patterdale terriers, but one thing which supports this rumour is that Middleton breeding, although black and tan, or red, does produce black progeny when put to black bitches. No doubt this gene for producing blacks has been inherited from Bedlington blood which played an important part in the creation of early Fell, and Lakeland, terrier strains.

Bill Brightmore, although a fan of black and tan and red Fell types, also kept blacks and these were incredible workers. Too hard for some, maybe, but superb workers nevertheless. These blacks of Brightmore's were a mix of black stuff, no doubt originally from Nuttall's line, and Middleton blood, which was used to improve type in the strain, making them more competitive at terrier shows which are still an important part of Cumbrian life. Brian Plummer interviewed Bill Brightmore for

A Middleton strain Lakeland in working condition. Stripped out, this dog is very much like Sid Wilkinson's Rock in type.

his book, *The Fell Terrier*, but did not include him, for, when he accompanied his interviewee out onto the bleak fells around Brough, Brightmore had little control over his charges, shouting in vain as they headed across the fells with their noses to the ground, and Plummer hated to see a dog that could not be controlled by its owner. Nevertheless, Bill Brightmore bred some superb working terriers during his lifetime, particularly black stuff, now known as Patterdale terriers.

During more recent years, black and red Patterdales have become increasingly popular as both show and working dogs. In fact, at many shows, Patterdales now outnumber even Jack Russells, but it is as workers that they are most popular, at the moment anyway. At the time of writing, terrier work is still legal and, it has to be said, a vital part of countryside management in their traditional role as hunters of vermin. But the fight to ban hunting with dogs will not go away and many are determined to see a ban become law before very long. I hope very much that these efforts, based on ignorance, lying propaganda and prejudice, will fail badly. If not, then the Patterdale will become nothing but a show and lapdog, like many of the pedigree breeds that have all but lost their working instinct.

Many have foresaken Jack Russells and more traditional Fell and Lakeland terriers, and have taken up working Patterdales instead, for many of these earth dogs are incredibly game and persistent workers and are more famous for their staying ability than anything else. Also, many are so game that they will finish reluctant foxes below ground, or will succeed in bolting a fox that, if pestered by a baying type of terrier, just wouldn't shift. And so their popularity continues to grow. Wendy Pinkney, once well known for her red and black and tan terriers, is now breeding Patterdale types that work very well indeed. Of course, her strain is already based on the old Buck/Breay bloodlines through the dogs of Jack Smith, Nuttall and Dave Roberts, and so blacks are easily produced by the use of a Black stud dog, for her strain already carries the genes that produce this black colouring. Her

Wendy Pinkney-bred terriers

terrier strain has had quite an impact on working terrier blood-lines in the past few years and it is well worth a little time examining her breeding programme.

Wendy grew up in the world of hunting and, although her father, Maurice Bell, obviously reared her into a world of hounds and terriers, it was Frank Buck who was to influence her views the most. Frank helped out when Maurice set up the Wensleydale foxhounds and Wendy spent much time with Buck, both talking terriers and hunting with them too. For her twelfth birthday present Wendy received a Fell terrier bitch which she named 'Tanner'. She was a leggy, narrow dog, but soon became a very useful worker to fox. The terrier 'lived in' and was the butt of much light-hearted banter, becoming known as the 'fireside' dog. A fox was marked to ground at Pennhill rocks and Wendy was asked to try her 'fireside' dog. Tanner quickly entered the earth and found her fox in no time at all, baying strongly and steadily and eventually succeeding in bolting her fox to the waiting pack. This was a good start to a very useful career for this bitch which was bred out of Oliver Gill's wonderful looker and worker, Beano, and Steve Perry's bitch, Judy, another superb worker. Beano was out of Jack Smith's famous Ranter, another wonderful looker and worker. Smith dug both foxes and badgers with this dog, which proved itself a great finder and stayer in a wide variety of earths up and down the country. In turn, it was a son of Wally Wild's Kipper that sired Ranter, so this dog was a grandson of Breay's Bingo. Smith's Mantle, another great working terrier, was the dam of Ranter, so this bitch, Tanner, was very well bred indeed and was a worthy choice for the foundation of a strain of working terrier.

Sadly, Tanner picked up some strychnine at around five years of age and she never quite got it together after that and she was retired early. She bred two litters to a descendant of Maurice Bell's Britt and Brian Plummer bought two puppies from one of the litters, giving Wendy a signed blank cheque for the two terriers; such was the worth that Plummer put on the offspring of Bell's most famous of terriers, Britt. However, it was the third mating that continued this line.

John Winch's Chase, a dog bred down from Hardasty's Turk, yet another superb looker and worker, sired a litter when put to Tanner and Wendy kept back a dog pup from this union. Ross was the result of this mating and he proved an exceptional worker, so exceptional, in fact, that Frank Buck used this terrier for several seasons with the West of Yore foxhounds, while, of course, Wendy would use him with the Wensleydale. Buck really took to this terrier and the dog returned his affection, for Wendy would find that her terrier sometimes went missing and she could be sure that he would turn up at Buck's house at Harmby, so she wasn't too worried. Buck bolted many foxes with this terrier for hounds, but Ross, during his sixth season, began to become too hard for working with a mounted pack and began seriously damaging his foxes. Nevertheless, he continued to be a useful terrier until retirement in old age. Ross was quite a looker too and he won several shows, including the Great Yorkshire show in 1986. Even as a veteran, 'an old Dalesman', he still kept his looks. I remember Ross well and he was a leggy, narrow dog, but much better looking than his dam, Tanner.

A terrier that could fulfill the expectations of a legendary terri-erman such as Frank Buck, just had to be used to continue Wendy's breeding programme and he was mated to Bully, a bitch which worked regularly with a hunt in Kent. From this mating came Wendy's red bitch, Fury. Fury was mated to Flak, one of the few terriers Wendy has ever bought in, a dog bred out of Ward's Bret and Suzi, and from this union came Fern, a smart bitch which won at the Great Yorkshire show in 1993. Fern became a very good finder, but Wendy didn't rate her much after that, for she was a little weak when it came to bolting reluctant foxes. She was not at all hard, preferring to stand off and bay at her quarry instead; a quality that would have suited many terriermen who did their digging in the low country. But the Wensleydale cover a tough landscape full of undiggable rock earths and so Fern was of little use in an earth of this type which housed a fox that refused to shift.

Fern was mated by Tanner, a dog sired by Ben, a Middleton bred terrier which was owned by Brian Fleming. Fleming was Middleton's digging partner for many years and Ben, a dog that won many shows, was a superb worker. Tanner's dam was a bitch named Tess who was owned by Charlie Ormond, she was sired by Cowen's Rock. Rock served with the Melbreak and, according to Middleton, was probably the best looking and working terrier that Cowen ever bred. The mating ' twixt Tanner and Fern produced Wendy's bitch, Briar. Briar was a very strong, good looking bitch which won several shows, but it was as a superb worker that she made her name.

Briar was of a type that Wendy favours for work. She was not too hard, but was pushy enough to shift the most stubborn of foxes. Qualities such as this are desirable in a hunt country such as that hunted by the Wensleydale pack, for many of the earths are undiggable, or would need an army to dig out, and then only after several days and with the use of explosives and earth movers. Reluctant foxes that a terrier cannot shift must then be left to run for another day – something that does not please a hill shepherd who is losing lambs to fox predation. At one spot, hounds marked a fox to ground and Wendy entered Fern into the rocky laybrinth.

Fern soon found her fox skulking in the dark passages underground and she began baying steadily at her fox. However, Reynard had found himself a good vantage point and he was not for moving, no matter how vociferous the terrier became. In the end, Wendy replaced Fern with her daughter, Briar, who went to her fox with fire aplenty, grabbing hold of it, pulling it off the shelf where it had commanded the situation, and finally bolted her quarry. These qualities suited Wendy and she would carry on her breeding programme through this bitch.

Wendy wanted to put a little more fire into her strain, however, and settled on a suitable stud dog for both Fern and Briar. Mettle, bred and owned by Dave Kitson, was the stud she settled on and he proved a wise choice, for, when put to Fern, he bred Mist. Mettle was descended from Dave Robert's Rip, an incredible working black and tan terrier that was bred out of Middleton stuff, through McCoy, a terrier owned by the late Paul Blackledge. McCoy was an incredible worker too, and Blackledge did much hard digging with this dog, a terrier that helped shape his reputation as a digging man. His lurchers, blue in colour, were also incredible fox killing machines. It was McCoy who sired Kitson's Mettle, and Mist, the puppy kept back from the union between Mettle and Fern, proved yet another superb worker.

During her first outing with hounds, Mist was put to ground on her very first fox, killing one below ground and bolting a second fox; an incredible feat for a newly entered terrier. Brian Fisher, the one-time area representative for the Fell and Moorland Working Terrier Club Mid Lancs area, who took over from me when I resurrected this area during the early nineties, was present at this hunt. And I can remember him telling me about this terrier and how she had killed a fox on her very first outing. She followed this by killing the next eight foxes she was entered to, but she did so without taking severe punishment in the process.

She became a truly wonderful finder in even the deep earths of the Wensleydale country, earths that are every bit as dangerous as the borrans found throughout the Lakes country.

The Wensleydale pack had been hunting a fox keenly, but they were now struggling to fathom the scent, which had begun to fade as they hunted across the lower pastures near Hawes. Hounds then came upon an old stone drain and began marking eagerly. Mist was put in and she soon came to a very tight spot where Wendy had to dig to her in order to help her get through. This accomplished, the bitch disappeared into the depths of the drain which, Wendy estimates, was around 100 yards in length. It also contained several offshoots and double drains, that is, one drain directly on top of another, in places, so it was a very difficult place for a terrier to fathom. However, with persistence, Mist eventually found her foxes, three of them in fact, and finally bolted all three to hounds. And all three were accounted for by the waiting pack. This was one of the most memorable of all the hunts Wendy has taken part in and she was most impressed with her young bitch, Mist.

No doubt Mist would have become a legend in her own lifetime, had she had the chance. Tragically, she was lost to ground in a nightmare limestone earth high up in the Dales after Wendy had loaned her to a follower of the Wensleydale foxhounds. Had she been present, or had Maurice been up with hounds at the time, the bitch would never have been allowed to enter such a place, for it was one of those earths best avoided. Some of these limestone dens have cracks and crevices, or even large holes, which plunge into the earth for great depths and a terrier falling into them has virtually no chance of being rescued. Sadly, many terriers have come to grief in such places. Just visit one of the caves of the North Yorkshire Dales and see the many crevices from which icy cold water plunges. These watercourses can swallow up an unwary terrier when working the rocky laybrinths that abound in such regions. Even the most careful of terriermen can lose an earth dog or two when regularly hunting a landscape of this kind.

The mating between Mettle and Briar now took place and from this union came Wendy's excellent working bitch, Nettle, very much a Patterdale in type, though she is harsh coated, rather than smooth. Nettle has proved a superb worker. Paul Stead, the terrierman for the Pennine foxhounds, told me of the abilities of this bitch. I had just completed a hard dig to my dog Fell, a son

Brock, owned by Barry and Danny Hill. A superb worker bred out of Nuttall/Gould stock.

of Wendy's Briar, and he had taken quite a bit of punishment from his fox, which was pretty untypical of him. For he could usually finish his fox without receiving serious bites, and it was Paul who helped me treat his wounds. He was impressed by Nettle and her abilities, even as a young, newly entered terrier.

These later terriers of this breeding seem to get better with each successive generation, Wendy believes, and two of the terriers she has bred have proven to be superb earth dogs, these being Vandal and Viper. Viper has served with the Ludlow in Shropshire under the expert guidance of Dave Finlay, one of the best terriermen this country has produced in recent years and one who has a wealth of experience at entering and working terriers.

Finlay has taken large hauls of foxes with Viper, though this dog is now back with Wendy, serving at the Golden Valley hunt where Will, her husband, is Huntsman. Viper is a hard dog, capable of killing a reluctant fox, and he is a stayer, but he works his foxes with sense. He does not have the 'grab hold anywhere and hang on no matter what' disposition which usually sees terriers having to be retired early after most of the teeth and several parts of the jaw have been taken off.

Vandal and Viper resulted from a union 'twixt Nettle and Codie, a dog out of Nick Stevens' Mick and Pie, a bitch bred out of Jack Smith's old strain. Smith's strain was descended from the Buck/Breay breeding programme and so Wendy's strain carries many lines back to the dogs of the two 'masters'. And so, if the term Patterdale terrier is to be used when it comes to describing the type of terrier which originated in Buck and Breay's kennels, at Leyburn and Kirkby Lonsdale, then the terriers of Wendy Pinkney certainly qualify for such a term, especially the black stuff she now favours. In fact, the terrier, Bully, who bred Fury, the dam of Fern, was out of Chippy and Nigger, two Nuttall bred terriers, so this is another line that goes back to the dogs of the originators of what are now known as Patterdale terriers.

I bought Fell from Wendy a few years ago after he had served for two seasons with the Pennine foxhounds, simply because she was overstocked at the time and was not registered as one of the official 'terriermen' with this hunt. So she just didn't have enough work for all of her terriers. He has proven an inspired choice indeed. Fell was not a hard dog at all when I bought him, but he had bolted quite a number of foxes during those two seasons. He did a third season for me and I found him to be a good finder and stayer, but he rarely 'mixed it' with his quarry. However, things began to change during the early part of his fourth season after John Hill's small Teckel bitch, Fatima, had found a fox in a dug-out rabbit hole and was baying at it for all she was worth.

Fell was loose and quickly shot into the earth, pushing past the tiny bitch and laying into his fox immediately, killing it in a few short moments. From then on, he never looked back and he can quickly finish any fox that refuses to bolt, though few will stand their ground before him. I spoke to Wendy about this and she said that some terriers in her strain do become harder as they get older, Ross being just one of the terriers to follow this pattern. After six seasons, Fell has not only proven himself a stayer during long digs, but he will close with his quarry and finish it – something that really comes in handy when a lamb-killing fox is to ground in an undiggable earth, from which it will not bolt.

One of the best hunts I have had with this dog was in a small valley, which lies close to where I live. Fell had flushed quite a large fox from a bramble patch above a small wood and he had gone away close on its brush. I awaited his return, but there was no sign of him after a good few minutes, so I began looking for him, heading for nearby earths where I was sure he would be. Sure enough, I found him in a den high up on the hillside at a very steep spot. I could see into the earth for about eight feet or so, and then the passage turned and I could hear Fell hard at his fox just a couple of feet further on.

He finished his quarry quickly and emerged. I then entered my bitch, Mist, a good steady baying terrier, and I could plainly hear her ragging the carcass. To dig to the fox would have meant taking a huge piece of that hillside away and using props to support the roof of the dig. But, now knowing that Reynard had been dealt with, and in prime sheep herding country, I was content to leave the carcass where it was. A terrier of such abilities is worth its weight in gold when it comes to keeping a shepherd happy, for, even if the fox refuses to bolt from an impossible earth, one can still account for the predator at large. Fell terriers, in fact, have been created for this very purpose. Both Buck and Breay bred many terriers that were capable of such feats and modern Patterdales produce many such workers.

Fell is bred out of Briar and Bracken, a dog bred by Wendy out of Flak and Sedge, the same Flak which bred Fern when mated to Fury. Sedge was also out of Tanner, the sire of Briar, and it was Tanner who was sired by Fleming's Ben, a top winning and working Lakeland of the Middleton breeding. Both Briar and Bracken were descended from Smith's Ranter, and so Fell carries several lines back to Buck and Breay stuff. In fact, he is very much of the type produced by both Buck and Breay; hard coated, strong and chunky, and with a decidedly Borderish look about him. Bracken, the sire of Fell, belongs to M. Potter and this dog was used on lamb-killing foxes with the Lunesdale foxhounds.

Why are many terriermen turning to Patterdales and forsaking the more traditional Fell terrier bloodlines, not to mention Jack Russells and Border terriers? To answer this question, one must go back to percentages. Middleton estimates that if a strain, or breed, of terrier is producing seventy-five per cent good working stock, then that strain can be considered very good and well worth continuing. I believe this to be an accurate estimation for Fell terriers and Russells, though this would be far less for Borders I am sure, but I also believe that the percentage for sound working Patterdales is far higher than this; at least ninety-five per cent and possibly more. Also, Patterdales tend to have more staying power and really put the pressure on their fox, which means that more reluctant foxes will be bolted.

While it is true that there are many of the more traditional Fell types that work every bit as well as Patterdale terriers (though, as Wendy Pinkney says, most of these will have much Buck/Breay breeding in their bloodlines), it is also true to say that Patterdales produce far more consistent numbers of working animals than do other breeds. This is for various reasons, but the main reason is that Fell terriers have become possibly more popular as show dogs, than working animals in recent years, and working ability has suffered. One only needs to look at pedigree breeds such as the Scottish strains, to come to this conclusion. The Scottish breeds were among the best in the world at one time, but very few would even sniff at a hole these days. I have also seen Fell terriers, when out with hounds, totally refuse to even look at a fox when the owner has been asked to try their terrier!

Many Fell terrier bloodlines are going the same way. Even Middleton's strain, once famed for its staying ability and its knack of finishing reluctant foxes, has suffered somewhat in the past few years, simply because many who keep and breed them just do not bother working their charges, though I must stress that

Ghyll, a red Patterdale bred by Bruce Hardy out of Parkes' stuff.

Gary still works his terriers to fox, doing most of his hunting in Yorkshire these days, and many of his terriers are just as good as the old stuff produced by the Barkers and the Wilkinsons. The hunting instinct will always suffer and grow weaker with each 'redundant' generation. The saying 'use it or lose it' is very true when it comes to working breeds of terrier. The fact that such a large percentage of Patterdale owners are working terrier enthusiasts, more concerned with how a dog performs to ground, rather than in the show ring, is the reason why such a high percentage of these terriers make good, and very often excellent, workers.

It is a similar story with Jack Russells too. At one time, and only a couple of decades back, most Russell owners worked them and so a high percentage would work. Nowadays, most owners show them, or simply keep them as pets, and working ability has suffered. If the Patterdale terrier becomes a popular show dog, and all the signs point to the fact that this is indeed the case, then this breed of terrier may well go the same way. At the moment though, although showing is becoming more popular, the vast majority, if not one hundred per cent, of the lads exhibiting are working terriermen, so there is no need to worry on that score. Let us hope that a hunting ban will not reduce the Patterdale to being a non-worker, no better than a pet Poodle. Talking of Poodles, maybe I am doing them an injustice, for these can be pretty game dogs, as I recently found out.

During those days when badger digging was legal and was carried out in a humane manner by true countrymen, Gary Middleton was taking part in a dig near his home and a Mrs Robinson appeared on the horizon with her pet Poodle. Middleton expected her to kick up a fuss (many were already turning against badger diggers as lying propaganda meant that the public could not differentiate between diggers and baiters) and so he awaited the barrage of abuse. But none came. Instead, the lady asked if her dog could have a go, for it was now doing cartwheels on the end of its lead, keen to join the other dog which was working its quarry keenly. Middleton had broken through to dog and badger and, just to keep her happy, and no doubt keen to see how a Poodle would handle such a situation, he agreed to allow it a minute or two while he cleared a space in order to tail his quarry. That Poodle flew into the earth, bayed at its quarry and seized it (badgers have very dense fur and thick skin, meaning that a dog bite will not penetrate), hanging on despite the protestations of 'Brock'. Many 'evangelise' about the courage of Poodles and this was certainly true in this case.

Middleton also tells a tale about a pedigree Corgi that took part in some gruelling fox digs around Appleby. Gary went digging up that way quite regularly at one time and a chap called Billy owned this Corgi which was very adept at killing reluctant foxes. In fact, Middleton stated that he has never seen a dog kill foxes as quickly as did this Corgi, its massively powerful head completing the job very swiftly indeed. Of course, Corgi types were introduced into this country by the ancient Celts three thousand years ago and these were undoubtedly used for hunting purposes. A herding breed has obviously been introduced in more recent times, possibly by Welsh farmers who wanted them to be more useful around the place (though more likely by show enthusiasts once the exhibiting craze had taken hold), but some Corgis still retain a terrier-like disposition and will go to ground.

Many modern terrier lads have turned to Patterdales because of the strong working instinct which runs consistently through these strains. Dave Harcombe, Dave Finlay, Wendy and Will Pinkney, Nick Stevens, Danny Sykes, Barry Wild, Steve Ellis and

Mist, out of Wild's black stuff, emerging from an earth after bolting a fox – which was too quick for me.

scores of others, are all making use of this type of working terrier. There is not the space in these pages to cover all of these terrier-men thoroughly, but one thing is certain; every modern Patterdale terrier, regardless of who owns it, will have at least some blood of the dogs of Brian Nuttall running in their veins. For Nuttall has been a prolific breeder of this type of terrier for at least the past forty years, though he was breeding and working terriers long before then. Nuttall is a fascinating man to talk to and his knowledge of different terrier breeds is incredible, for, at the age of seventy, he can remember the terriers that were around before the days of exaggerated furnishings ruined many breeds of once outstanding working terriers.

I asked him about the terriers of Buck and Breay and his tales of those two are fascinating. Nuttall, of course, hunted with both Buck and Breay and he has fond memories of his times spent with them. Mr Breay and his father, a vicar, brought with them to Mallerstang a strain of working Sealyham terrier that originated in South Wales and these had been used extensively for badger digging, as Breay was a very keen badger digger during his younger years. Even as an old man, Cyril Breay still enjoyed seeing a game terrier at work and Middleton took him on a dig in the Winster valley just before he died. Of course, the old man was far too frail to join in, but, nevertheless, he much appreciated seeing terriers at work for what was probably the last time before he finally succumbed to a long illness.

These Sealyham terriers were wonderfully game dogs, but Breay found them unsuited to the northern earths of the area he had settled in. Being reluctant to lose the working instinct of these dogs, however, he mated them to Fell terriers and created his own strain of working terrier that was well suited to the terrain he now hunted. I asked Nuttall about Bull terrier blood and whether he thought that Buck and Breay had used such blood in their strain. He went on to say that most terriers of those early days had quite a bit of Bull terrier about them, though he was quick to stress that these were not the bulky Staffordshire terriers, but far smaller and lighter fighting dogs that only weighed in at sixteen or eighteen pounds.

I told him about Frank Buck taking a pied Bull terrier with him on those badger digs that were organised by Mr and Mrs Williams (Brian also knew this family quite well), and whether he thought that the use of this terrier was a possibility. I could see by the look on his face that something had clicked when I told him of what my research had uncovered. Most Buck/Breay terrier enthusiasts totally dismiss any suggestion of this pair using Bull terrier blood in their strain, but I found Nuttall's honesty refreshing, for he then went on to say that Frank Buck sent some terriers to Lancashire many years ago (to the Rossendale valley in fact which is a hard land on any type of working terrier, being full of old mines and disused quarries where rockpiles abound) that showed both a Bull terrier influence and the pied colouring which is typical of Bull blood. Others were of a black brindling in colour.

Two of these were Mick and Grip, two Buck-bred dogs which displayed Bull terrier and the pied colouring of such a cross. I have only just talked to Nuttall about this and had already written down the four options found in the previous chapter. In the light of what Nuttall said, I can only conclude that this pied Bull terrier was indeed tested as to gameness and was then

(*left to right*) Piper, Kiwi, Coffee and Racket; Nuttall-bred Patterdales.

brought into the Buck/Breay project, the selective breeding programme then producing very typey and ultra-game terriers such as Bingo, Rusty and Ripple. Mr Breay knew of genetics and he could so easily have bred out any faults inherited from such a cross in a relatively short time, though for quite a few generations he had problems with terriers which lacked sense. These would grab a fox anywhere and hang on for dear life, taking terrific punishment as a consequence.

Nuttall began working his grandfather's strain of terrier which carried several lines back to small fighting Bull terriers that were common throughout the North-east of England (though dogs of this type were found throughout the country at one time) and these dogs were very game indeed, as one can imagine. Nuttall then took his bitches to Buck and Breay bred terriers and thus the famous Nuttall strain of Patterdale terrier, a strain that has influenced all other strains of black Patterdale terriers up and down the country, began.

Nuttall was quick to stress that, although Frank Buck played an important part in the breeding of what later became known as the Patterdale terrier, it was Mr Breay who started the strain and it was Mr Breay who 'masterminded' it, so to speak. Buck's Tiger, for instance, was bred out of a Breay bred bitch and a dog owned by Breay. And it was Mr Breay who introduced Frank to the world of working terriers when he gave Buck a dog named Tickler, bred out of the old Sealyham/Fell bloodlines. Nevertheless, Frank became a top class terrierman who was both a top breeder of working stock and a man who treated his quarry in a humane manner. Roger Westmoreland, who dug with both Buck and Breay from the late fifties onward, was quick to stress how Buck showed great respect for the quarry he hunted. Frank Buck also produced some very typey dogs later on, but it was Breay's knowledge of genetics which had provided the foundation for such good looking stock, for Breay won many shows with his dogs and, as Middleton stated, knew how to produce typey stock which won well at shows, but also worked well in the field.

Brian Nuttall took his bitches to Black Davey, Rusty and Wally Wild's Kipper, and from then on has bred from his own dogs, or dogs that have been bred out of his stock. There is a hint of Border terrier in the strain, but very little. He will not use a dog that is not at least three quarters bred from his own bloodlines, and that is how Border blood got into the strain; from a dog which had just one quarter Border breeding in its bloodlines. A dash of outcross blood is necessary in any strain, in order to increase the gene pool, but he would not put in any stud dog unless at least three quarters bred to his own stock, as I have stated, and then only if it is a proven, consistent and sensible worker. In fact, he will not breed from any dog or bitch until it has proven game to fox. This is commendable, especially in a world now obsessed with the show dog when stud dogs and brood bitches are used at the earliest opportunity, long before they have proven themselves to be capable of sticking at their work throughout at least one season.

Nuttall never breeds for show, though some of the terriers that crop up in his litters are very typey and would do well in the show ring. He laments the fact that pedigree blood has been used on many working terrier strains in order to produce show stock, for both the temperaments and the qualities needed in a working terrier are ruined by such bloodlines. He also mentioned how many showy type Fell terriers are now being produced which are as light as a feather and would blow away in even a moderate wind, let alone a strong gale. For a terrier to stand its ground against a fox, even a small vixen, it must have some weight behind it, especially if it is going to hold its quarry until dug out. I picked up some of Brian's terriers and, though a shade on the small side, these had plenty of substance.

Many are put off by the size of Nuttall's terriers and I believe this to be a mistake. True, they are only small, anywhere between ten and twelve inches in the main, but, as I have stated, they have much substance about them and they are also very strong little dogs, with very good heads. His grandfather's strain had very strong heads, as did the dogs of Buck and Breay, and this influence can clearly be seen in the terriers of Brian Nuttall. Brian believes that size really doesn't matter, for it is the sense that counts with terriers. If an earth dog works its fox cleverly, dodging the attack, but working its quarry hard and keeping the pressure on, then Nuttall believes that any terrier with a bit of substance to it, whatever its size, can work a fox successfully and come out of the encounter without too much damage. The terrier that shoots into an earth and gets stuck into its fox, receiving much punishment in the process, is not for Brian. Sense is rated very highly by this man, for he requires a dog to be capable of being worked several times a week if necessary and one that is constantly having to be rested until it heals is of no use to him at all.

Nuttall much prefers blacks and his strain is predominantly of this colour, though chocolates do crop up in the litters from time to time. Others are of a very attractive bronze colour. Some refer to these as chocolates, but this is an inaccurate description as a true chocolate will also have a chocolate nose, while the bronze coloured dogs have a typical black nose. Although many attribute this chocolate colour to the influence of Bedlington blood of earlier times (much sturdier, hardy terriers more akin to Dandie Dinmonts than modern pedigree Bedlingtons), Nuttall believes this colouration to be a natural result of the breeding of black and red terriers. There is much substance in this, of that I have no doubt, but the truth is that Bedlington blood did enter many Fell and Lakeland strains and chocolate puppies resulted from this influence. Bedlington blood certainly entered the Buck/Breay breeding programme through Tink for one, the sire of Tiger, but I suspect that Bedlington blood entered through other terriers of this strain too, for Fell terrier bloodlines were heavily saturated with such blood during the earlier part of the twentieth century.

Brian prefers smooth coats as these are easily cleaned and they do not collect huge balls of mud, ice, or snow. He does not like to see a smooth coat of the type found on an Italian Greyhound, however, for such a jacket gives very little protection to a dog working in extreme mid-winter conditions, resulting in them chilling badly, especially if they spend hours on end inside a freezing drainage pipe, or a rock earth. Middleton, among others, will not tolerate anything less than an iron-hard rough coat, but Nuttall is satisfied with a smooth coat, as long as it is dense and lies closely knit to the skin. Such a jacket does indeed keep the weather out, but whether it is as effective at giving protection as the harsh Irish terrier-type jacket will no doubt be a matter of debate for many years to come.

I have seen Plummer terriers (which have similar jackets to Nuttall bred Patterdales) working in ice-cold winds on the Isle of North Uist in the Outer Hebrides, being sprayed by the Atlantic sea, and they have not shown the slightest bit of discomfort. However, how such dogs would cope if they were trapped in a large rockpile on the side of a steep fell in the middle of winter when the land is gripped in an iron-hard frost, is a question I cannot answer. One thing I do know; terriers with that harsh jacket have stood up to the severest of weather conditions, sometimes being trapped in a borran for days on end amongst the cold stone, which gives no warmth at all to the captive, while others have died of shock, or have suffered very badly from the cold and wet. I know of smooth-coated terriers that have been stuck fast in a rockpile during a period of hard frost which have died of the cold overnight, though this is a rare occurrence it has to be said. After several decades of working smooth terriers in all types of terrain up and down the country, Nuttall still seems more than happy with a smooth jacket, so there can't be that much wrong with such a coat!

However, although he has a preference for smooths, rough coats do appear in litters from time to time and there was a small number with this type of jacket when I visited his kennels in Cheshire. If anything, most of these just develop a rough jacket around the head, but one dog he had in kennel was quite a typey terrier which was not unlike the type produced by Black Davey, a superb worker that was bred by Breay and owned by Buck, a dog which Brian used as one of the foundation studs for his own strain of terrier. In fact, this dog was very much like the later stuff Buck was breeding after the death of Mr Breay; small rough coated black terriers which won well at shows and worked well also, bolting foxes for local packs of hounds, particularly the Bedale and the West of Yore, though Buck's terriers worked with many different packs throughout the country. Even though it is many years since Nuttall used a Buck or Breay bred terrier, the characteristics continue to crop up in these litters. This is only possible if one 'locks in' the qualities so desired in a terrier, just as Middleton succeeded in doing with Wilkinson's Rock.

Nuttall usually enters his terriers straight to foxes. He hunted mink quite a lot at one time, but doesn't bother much with this type of quarry these days. He will start a terrier at eleven or twelve months of age, but will have allowed his youngsters to rag a fox carcass, or a brush, before entering begins. If at all possible, he likes to give a youngster a nice easy dig to begin with. Of course, we cannot pick and choose the earths foxes will use, so sometimes a longer dig is inevitable. This matters not at all though, as long as the youngster gains confidence during the proceedings.

A long dig will, for the most part, see a more experienced dog doing most of the work and the young entry will be allowed to join in towards the end, for he does not believe in over-facing an apprentice. Nor does he believe in allowing a terrier to go to ground at too young an age. He knows of some who allow a pup of around eight months to go to a fox and there is no better way

A brace of hardworking Patterdale Terriers; renowned for their gameness and versatility.

of ruining a terrier than by giving it too tough a task early on in its training. His advice to any who have put a terrier to fox at such a young age is to leave it until about eighteen months, and then try it again. Just maybe they will get away with it and the terrier will not have been damaged by the encounter.

Others of his strain will not face a fox at even twelve months of age. If this refusal to work occurs, Brian simply leaves the youngster until it is eighteen months of age and then tries again. He was quick to stress that he has no failures using this method. In fact, Brian guarantees his stock will work, but only if entered properly. If those who purchase puppies just follow his advice – not to enter a puppy too early and to give it more simple tasks during the first few encounters, and leaving a youngster until it reaches the age of eighteen months if it refuses to go at a year – then he is confident there will be no failures. Personally, I do not agree with this, for no strain of terrier can produce a one hundred per cent success rate, no matter what the methods of entering are employed, but I get his point. If those who work terriers were more patient and allowed the dog to develop at its own pace, encouraging and praising it along the way, then there would be very few failures. I believe a success rate of at least ninety-five per cent is a more realistic view, for the author has come across failures in the very best of strains, despite the fact that they have been given every opportunity to develop into good workers. The Nuttall strain is among the very best, but still, I do not believe, in an imperfect world, that a one hundred per cent success rate is possible.

I suppose it depends on the standards one sets for what qualifies as a working terrier. If one is happy to have terriers that do a bit of bushing, flushing rabbits, digging out rats along hedgerows and bolting the occasional fox, then yes, a one hundred per cent success rate would be possible. But if, like Nuttall and many other first-rate terriermen, one requires earth dogs to find in any type of earth, no matter how deep or vast, to engage the fox and bolt it, or stay until dug out, then I believe it would be asking too much of any strain, no matter how good, to consistently produce dogs that can match this standard to a one hundred per cent rate.

Brian Nuttall will take, on average, about thirty foxes each season. At one time, and not so long ago it has to be said, he would take about seventy foxes each season, but there are that many people now shooting them on the lamp that far fewer are around. Coupled with milder winters, which means that many foxes are now living above ground all year round, then this means that it is increasingly difficult to find foxes inhabiting their earths. Unless one works terriers in conjunction with hounds, far fewer foxes will be taken these days. The trouble is, as Middleton said, 'there are a million people out with hounds and three million terriers'. An exaggeration, yes, but the point is that, even if you have the best terriers in the world, it is a lottery which ones are used on a hunt day, for there are always plenty for a Huntsman to choose from.

Although Middleton has hunted with several packs, including the Ullswater alongside Sid Wilkinson and Anthony Barker, and has used his terriers with such hunts, most of his digging has been done privately. He spent most of his time in the Ullswater country when Barker and Wilks were alive and still very actively involved in terriers and their work, but they would often hunt on their own, away from hounds, usually shifting badgers for farmers and hill shepherds, simply because there were far too many out with the hunt who were keen to get their terrier to ground before anyone else. And anyway, Gary had far too much work on at the time, shifting foxes and badgers for troubled landowners, so very little time could be spared for following hounds.

The shooting of foxes while lamping, or the taking of foxes with lurchers after calling them in, is on the increase and I know of several farms where large hauls have been taken in just a few weeks, almost a score in some cases. Fox control is absolutely necessary, true, but I cannot help but feel that some are out to massacre, rather than control, the fox population. I have noticed a definite decline in fox numbers over the past couple of years, and others are reporting the same. In this situation, it may be prudent for terrier lads to release the foxes they dig, unharmed. As long as a terrier is allowed to taste the occasional carcass and is given plenty of praise and encouragement, this will do no harm at all to a working terrier.

If a terrier feels it is pleasing its master then it will work just as keenly as a terrier allowed to taste the carcass of every fox taken. In fact, Nuttall kills few foxes, preferring to release them in order to keep enough foxes for his dogs to work. He is especially adamant that cubs should not be dug, unless, of course, lambs and other livestock are being taken by the dog fox and vixen. John Settle of Todmorden, a good terrier and lurcher man by any standards, shares this same view. When I was speaking to him he knew of three litters of cubs within easy reach of his home, yet he left them strictly alone; a commendable attitude in this day and age. The fool who hunts during the springtime when it is unnecessary to do so, is only killing off the future work for his dogs. Of course, sometimes one comes upon cubs by accident and there is nothing one can do to stop your terrier from killing them, but that is different to going out to deliberately hunt them down.

I came upon a litter of cubs only a couple of years ago, by accident, and the terriers were loose at the time, so there was nothing I could do to stop them. I was out walking in a valley close to my home when Mist and Fell began sniffing around piles of builders' rubble that had been so thoughtlessly dumped there. I thought they were after rats, but Fell disappeared and began baying keenly. Shortly afterwards, he emerged and Mist shot into the rubble, but soon emerged, dragging a dead fox cub as she came. She shot in again and returned with another cub, and then a third. The vixen and dog fox were nowhere to be seen (if one disturbs an earth with cubs inside, the vixen will usually stand a short distance away and bark for her cubs to join her) and I was puzzled as to why they should leave them in such a shallow, easily accessible spot with very little protection. I will never hunt during the spring, unless a farmer is being troubled.

Many years ago I used to hunt with a chap called Roy and he had permission on several farms where he did much of the maintenance on farm machinery. One day during April, at a time when I dislike hunting, for I strongly believe in a closed-season when nature can get on with replenishing the land, we went out with the terriers to a spot high on the moors where the shepherds always have problems with foxes (and badgers) preying on their lambs. It didn't take long to find the breeding earth, which was inside a rockpile on the edge of a quarry. It was quite mild and spring-like down in the low country, but up there on the top of the moors winter was still well and truly with us, the icy winds making the going difficult as we crossed the rough ground.

I was entering my bitch, Rock, at the time. She had taken part in a few digs alongside Pep, and was learning fast, but this was more serious stuff, for these foxes had to be dealt with, whether we could dig to them or not. Rockpiles can be incredibly difficult and awkward places for digging down to a terrier, so we decided to enter Rusty, a Buck/Breay bred terrier of the type produced by Breay's famous dog, also called Rusty, though our terrier was not quite as strongly built as the more typical dogs of this strain. Barry Hill of Lancashire, a close friend of Clifford Yates, who is a cousin of Brian Nuttall, owned this dog for many years and he picked him up at a dog's home. Despite the mystery of his breeding it was obvious that he was out of this most famous of terrier strains. How he ended up at a dog's home, I do not know, but I guess he was put to ground and assumed trapped. Then, when the owner went off to get help, or went home for the night without bothering to block him in, believing the dog to be unable to get out by himself anyway (a common mistake), the terrier then emerged and wandered off. He was eventually picked up by someone and ended up in the home, the former owner no doubt believing him to be lost forever in the depths of the earth. The same thing happens to scores of terriers each year.

Rusty proved a superb worker, a great finder and a dog that could bolt a reluctant fox, or finish it below ground should it refuse to shift. He didn't have a particularly large head, but he had a good strong head typical of the Buck/Breay breeding programme, together with the slape coat. Rusty entered the rockpile eagerly, with Rock on his heels (although it is unwise to put two terriers to ground in most earths, especially tight dug-out rabbit holes where the second terrier can push the first straight into the fox, or even attack the rear end of the dog in front, it is sometimes necessary in a large rockpile) and they were soon at their foxes. With all of the remains and scats outside this earth, it was obvious that the cubs were well grown and so, just in case the vixen bolted (vixens are diligent mothers, but, like doe rats, will leave their youngsters once they are up and around, when danger threatens) I had Merle posted closeby, for it would not go down too well if any escaped in such a landscape where quarrying and sheep farming were the only means of making a living.

Despite the fact that the two terriers were working their foxes hard, none bolted. After giving them plenty of time to settle, it was decided to begin digging, though this wasn't going to be easy with all of those large slabs of rock in the way. We assessed the situation and decided that the best way of tackling this job was to dig into the hillside, rather than digging down from the top. Operations began and the terriers continued to bay at and tackle their quarry.

The first couple of feet was fairly easy going, being made up mainly of clay soil and small rocks, but it wasn't long before we started hitting the big stuff. By digging around these larger rocks and loosening them after much effort, it was possible eventually to move them out of the way. Things continued like this for much of the day until the onset of darkness forced us down from the hill. We blocked the terriers in thoroughly and would return at first light with more digging tackle, and hopefully more lads. We had managed to get a few feet into this earth by now, but the going was slow because of all those large boulders which took quite a bit of time and effort to shift. A decent sized tunnel was now taking shape and, thankfully, no roof props would be needed as the huge slabs of rock above our heads were well supported by even more large rocks which we were digging around, getting ever nearer to those baying sounds.

I went to my local that night in order to conscript reinforcements and I was relieved that a couple of friends, Nick and Lee, agreed to come early next morning. Sure enough, Nick and Lee were at my house first thing and it wasn't long before we found ourselves climbing that steep moor once again with the heavy digging tackle under our arms and on our shoulders.

We soon reached the earth, but there was complete silence from within, though it was difficult to hear anything because of the strong, cold winds buffeting the rocks all around. I unblocked the entrance and shouted for the terriers to come. We could then hear them whining and soon realised that this was now turning into a terrier rescue. They had obviously finished their quarry, but were now trapped, probably because a carcass was blocking their exit.

Digging operations began in earnest and the five of us made good progress until, by lunchtime, we were around fifteen feet into the hillside, with quite a few more large rocks having been taken out of the way. Some of these were so large and heavy that all we could do was to slowly shuffle them out of the earth. This took quite a lot of time and effort, but it was well worthwhile, for a large space had been cleared and a great deal of progress made with each large rock we succeeded in shifting. I took a bolster and heavy hammer along in order to crack some of the larger rocks, but this was incredibly difficult going and not very successful, so we gave up in the end and stuck to other methods which were far more effective.

Just as I was sitting down to eat lunch, another member of the team having taken my place in the tunnel, Rock emerged from

Patterdales are full of life and inquisitiveness.

the entrance, turned and was about to go back, when I grabbed her and secured her on the couples. She had a few small bites, from well-grown cubs, around her lips and on her nose, but otherwise she was fine. We called to Rusty, but he didn't follow and we could still hear him whining. In fact, we were now very close to the spot and he could be heard clearly only a couple of feet away at the most. The trouble was, there were huge boulders in our way and there was no way of either shifting them, or digging around them. Our digging operations had gone as far as they possibly could, from this angle anyway. We decided to start digging down from the top, though this was going to be far more difficult. There was nothing else for it. A few other lads were on the way, which was a good thing for we were just about done in, but still, I decided to go and telephone the area rep for the Fell and Moorland Working Terrier Club who was Paul Blackledge at the time, for this dig was going to take an enormous effort, and some machinery no doubt, if it was to be successful.

On my return, to my great relief, Rusty had also managed to get free of the earth and he showed signs that he had dealt with the vixen. Taking a family of foxes is never pleasant, but must be done when farmers are losing lambs. One or two may be acceptable, but a fox will rarely stop at one or two. If left unchecked, fox predation can take up to thirty lambs from just one farm during the early spring and this is totally unacceptable, for it is hard enough scraping a living from the land without allowing predators to take as much stock as they like. I have never been proud of hunting foxes during springtime, but this activity is essential, more especially in these hard times for the farming community.

Brian Nuttall will engage in this activity if called upon to do so, but otherwise, like all true countrymen, will leave foxes strictly alone once the winter hunting is finished. He has had some superb working terriers over the many years he has kept them. Some of the bitches have been outstanding, but he has consistently produced top working dogs, which he uses to keep the bloodlines alive, though only after they have proven themselves at work. Tarmac, Granite, Punch, Blitz 2, Miner and Gripper are just a few of the top working stud dogs he has had. Miner died a couple of years ago, but he made quite a name for himself and he has sired many top working Patterdale terriers. Gripper is another well-known name among the terriers of Brian Nuttall and he sired two superb workers belonging to Graham Hill and

Clifford Yates. These terriers have proven themselves working some difficult spots around the Lancashire countryside.

Many of Brian's terriers are loaned out each season to different hunts. Shamrock (now answering to Shammy after Edmond Porter called her by this name) has spent two seasons with the Eskdale and Ennerdale. Other hunts which use Nuttall bred

Brian Nuttall
with Patterdale
terriers.

terriers include the Carmarthen and the Blackmore Vale and Brian will have as many as twelve terriers out on loan during most seasons, for he cannot find enough work for all of the terriers he keeps. He can always find good blood to breed from, however, for his terriers are working throughout the length and breadth of Britain and he has sent quite a number of dogs to other countries such as Ireland and America.

Brian Nuttall must be considered as *the* most important breeder of modern Patterdales as the blood of his terriers laid the foundation for by far the majority of black stuff that is around today. Gould's Smithy was partly Nuttall bred and this terrier has given rise to a dynasty of typey black terriers. Smith's Ranter was mostly Nuttall bred too. Many supposed that Ranter had pedigree blood in his lines, he was that smart, but Nuttall stated that the bitch who bred Ranter always threw typey stock, despite the fact that Brian *never* breeds for show. In fact, any breeder of black stuff today would struggle not to find the dogs of Brian Nuttall in the bloodlines of their terriers, whether they think of them as Patterdales or not.

It was Nuttall who fixed type in these terriers, for Buck bred his own small strain of hard coated blacks which he used as hunt terriers, while Mr Breay, when he died in the early seventies, left a kennel of red terriers, some smooth, others rough, of differing types. Although there is other blood in these dogs, such as the strain bred by Nuttall's grandfather, the influence of Buck/Breay terriers still remains strong in these bloodlines. Certainly Nuttall, though not the originator of what are now referred to as Patterdales, can be thanked for preserving a type of terrier that is extremely game and useful in all types of earth. They do not suit everybody, for they would do very badly in the show ring today, but as working terriers they take some beating. They have been tested throughout the land in every type of earth known to man and one thing is for sure, these Patterdale terriers have not been found wanting.

Another of the more important breeders of black terriers is Barry Wild of Rochdale. Barry believes that the term Patterdale terrier should apply to the old strains of unregistered Lakeland terrier and he stated that Middleton's strain are the true Patterdale, as they are descended from dogs bred and worked in this region of Cumbria. In fact, he does not consider his dogs to be either Patterdales, or black Fell terriers, but simply black Lakelands. The truth of the matter is, however, that anything black is now referred to as a Patterdale, or a black Fell terrier, but never as a Lakeland.

Barry started out with terriers at the age of nine years when he obtained his first dog – a Staffordshire Bull terrier cross Jack Russell which he used for hunting rats and rabbits. At the age of sixteen he switched to the hunting of foxes, accompanying friends of his who were taking part in fox shoots, flushing and driving foxes to waiting guns, or bolting them from earths with terriers and shooting them as they attempted to escape. The Rochdale hunt was still going then and they would hunt the hares on the same land where these fox drives took place. He stated that these shooting men took any type of dog along and these were used, even mongrels, for bolting and flushing foxes. In fact, Barry has seen quite a number of mongrel terrier types which made into superb finding and bolting dogs.

The first terrierman to make an impression on the young Barry Wild was the late Billy Gammon who got his terriers from a game-keeper who lived in the Glossop area; black terriers which were superb workers. Barry cannot remember how they were bred, but believes they were probably from Buck/Breay stock (which terriers weren't in those days?), and it was these dogs which started his passion for black terriers, though, strangely enough, his next terrier, the first of note, was a red bitch which he bought direct from Cyril Breay. This bitch, Tess, was ten months old when Barry bought her and Breay said that he would take a pound for each month of her life, so she cost Barry ten pounds. He bought her from the Bramham Moor show in 1969, a show Breay always attended, and he took her out the very next day. She was unentered at the time of purchase, but that was about to change.

Barry took her to a large rockpile at Wardle and there were plenty of signs of fox, in fact, the smell of fox was so strong that he could taste it in his mouth. He was certain Reynard was at home, but the bitch kept entering the earth and then returning soon after. With persistence, however, after about fifteen times of sending her back in, something clicked in the bitch and she began going deeper and at last began growling and then baying. After two hours the bitch fell silent, but Barry continued to dig, a dig that lasted for four hours, and finally came upon his bitch; she had killed her fox deep inside the earth. For a terrier to finish her first fox at just ten months of age is a sign of real quality; such were the terriers bred by the two 'masters', Cyril Breay and Frank

Buck. Tess, as you can imagine, is where the strain bred by Barry Wild began.

Tess was a slape coated bitch and was typical of what are now known as Patterdale terriers, though they were being labelled by this name while Breay was still alive. Tess was mated to another slape coated dog, a black terrier bred by Ken Gould which was purchased by a friend, another tremendous worker, for work was the only thing Wild bred for at the time and it wasn't until the age of twenty-three that he began breeding much more seriously. At this time the very best bloodlines were to be found at the kennels of Gary Middleton of Kendal and so Wild began using the stud dogs of this breeding to put to his bitches which were very much of the old stuff bred by Cyril Breay and Frank Buck. This stuff just wasn't typey enough for Barry, for he began attending shows far more seriously and now wanted terriers to be more pleasing to the eye, though working qualities were still every bit as important as they always were.

Barry believes that Gary Middleton did all of the hard work for the terriermen that would come after him, for he had bred from the very best bloodlines in the Lakes, blood that would have now been lost, had he not done so, Barry believes, and was producing the very best looking and working stock in the country; stock that could handle a badger throughout a lengthy dig, and finish a fox should it refuse to bolt, terriers, in fact, of the traditional Lakeland type. Wild used Rex on his bitches, old Rex which was used by both Dave Roberts and Ken Gould, and began breeding much more typey stuff than previously, though it was stuff which worked incredibly well too, for Rex was possibly the gamest terrier ever to come out of the Lakes country and Barry dug to this dog on many occasions. He confirmed what Middleton had already told me, stating that this dog could utterly dominate even a large boar badger (this was when it was legal to dig badgers) and that he killed foxes easily, very casually. Rex had a massive head and no fox could stand against him should they have been foolish enough not to bolt.

While out with Dave Roberts, Rex was put into a badger sett and he began working his quarry with the usual fire, bolting eight badgers from the earth and bottling up a ninth, which Roberts and Wild then dug out. When they came upon the terrier, he had throttled his quarry in the hole-end. This, I know, is hard to believe, but Middleton had already told me of a dig in the Winster valley he took part in when Rex was to ground on badger. When

Middleton broke through, the badger was dead, having been throttled by Rex. Middleton stated that the badger may have had a bad heart and the dog working it simply brought on heart failure, but Wild is adamant that Rex killed, not just one badger, but a few during digs with Dave Roberts, by grabbing them by the throat and throttling them. Barry saw this with his own eyes on more than one occasion and this was just one of the reasons why he used Rex to 'polish up' his own strain of working terrier.

The dogs of Bill Brightmore – black stuff that was smartened up with the use of Middleton stock – were also used in those early days, to put in the more dominant black genes and keep this colour alive, but working instinct was also maintained by such blood, as the dogs of Brightmore's, though typey enough to compete at shows, were first and foremost workers. Wild has dug with Bill Brightmore on several occasions and told of the abilities of these terriers. Barry also used Dave Roberts' famous terrier, Rip, which may have been partly Middleton bred. Rip was an outstanding worker and many modern blacks are descended from him, though he was a black and tan. Roberts got into black stuff and Rip served many bitches, much of the progeny coming black and founding a dynasty of hard working terriers.

When interviewing Brian Nuttall I asked him about the term Patterdale terrier and if it was he who first began applying this name to the red and black terriers which originated with Breay and Buck of Cumbria and North Yorkshire. He quickly skirted the subject by saying that the name has always been used, but the truth is it has not always been used with reference to the modern type, but was applied to the old Lakeland which gave rise to the pedigree Lakeland terrier. I asked Barry Wild if he knew when and where this 'labelling' began. He is adamant that Buck and Breay terriers first began being named Patterdales around the Rossendale valley area (Lancashire) many years ago, while Breay was still alive, probably sometime during the sixties, but he could not pinpoint who it was that first used the term. No doubt it was a collective group of terrier enthusiasts in this area who first began calling them Patterdales, for, as Barry stated, many lads from this area travelled up to Harmby and bought several dogs from Frank Buck, bringing them back to Lancashire where they were used for badger digging and killing foxes in the many undiggable earths of this region. Nuttall originally comes from the Rossendale valley, but I am not suggesting that it was he who first began using this term!

Barry also confirmed that several of these terriers were black brindle and brindle and white in colour and that they had a decided Bull terrier look about them. In fact, he stated that Tess, the bitch he bought direct from Breay, also showed obvious Bull terrier ancestry. Barry Wild not only saw these terriers for himself, but he also dug with some of them and he said that, on breaking through, the terrier would have a fox by the leg, or some other part of its body which left the punishing jaws free to inflict severe injury. At this time, Plummer was also digging to Buck/Breay bred terriers, as was Gary Middleton, and they say exactly the same thing. Again, all of this confirms that the Bull terrier taken along by Frank Buck and Cyril Breay on those digs organised by Mr and Mrs Williams, was indeed used as an outcross many years ago. Barry also stated that he would not use Buck stud dogs, not because of working ability which could not be faulted, except for a lack of sense in some cases, but because many had white blazes (some of these were small, while others were large) on their chest, or had large patches of white on their legs, and Barry aimed to breed pure blacks. He said that some Buck/Breay bred terriers he saw had one leg almost completely white. He hates to see any white at all on a black dog. He also stated that some of Bill Brightmore's blacks had a slight brindling in their jackets, and Brightmore certainly used terriers from both Buck and Breay. I believe the question as to whether or not Buck and Breay used Bull terrier blood has now been answered!

Although there is much of the original blood of Frank Buck and Cyril Breay in the bloodlines of Wild's terriers, the sharp lines and excellent general type have been brought about with the use of quite a few Middleton stud dogs, but these have been from among both his top lookers and, more importantly, his top workers. And so Barry produces a few reds and black and tans in his line, which one would expect from such breeding, though they are mostly black. One of his more recent members of the strain is a dog named Printer who killed his first fox at the age of just eight months. Another of his terriers was recently entered into a drain, a long, two hundred feet affair that the terrier scrambled up in search of its fox.

The dog fell silent and Barry told his son to block the dog in and they would return in order to dig it out. Barry stated that he does not breed baying terriers, but dogs that will quickly kill their quarry. If the reader is ever up that way, just take a little detour to the moors around Rochdale and one will soon understand why. This land is full of earths that could not possibly be dug and a terrier must account for its fox should it refuse to bolt. On their return, Barry lit the interior of the drain with a torch and he could see his dog pulling something. Eventually, the terrier reached the entrance and pulled out a large fox which it had finished and then drawn out. This is the type of working stuff that is needed in the North of England where foxes can find themselves a good vantage point and easily boss a terrier that will not 'mix it'. Fell terriers were originally bred for such purposes and Barry believes in keeping up the tradition.

During the early years of Barry's 'apprenticeship' with working terriers Frank Buck was doing a lot of judging and Wild admits that he learnt a lot from this legendary man, for Buck was a straightforward sort of chap who told it like it was. Barry had been digging badgers in Derbyshire with Dave Roberts and they had dug two or three which they later released unharmed; at the request of the landowner (Wild rarely killed badgers and always released them uninjured, unless the landowner requested otherwise). After the dig was over, Barry went to a show that afternoon and Buck was judging. On seeing the dog and the injuries it had received, Buck told Wild to get out of the ring and take the dog home immediately, adding that he must get it cleaned up, fed and placed in front of the fire as soon as possible. Barry complied (few people would argue with Buck, especially as he was usually right in what he said) and took his terrier home, realising what an idiot he had been. He would never again attempt to show an injured terrier – an admirable resolve in this world when some terriers are picked out at shows simply because they are badly scarred! Frank Buck would not have a terrier in the ring if it had any unhealed wounds whatsoever. Buck was a very humane man who treated both the terriers he hunted with, and the quarry he hunted, with great respect. Youngsters, even experienced lads, can learn much from the example of such men.

Black Solo and Black Crag were two stud dogs which Barry later brought into his strain. These were bred and worked by A. Chapman of Wales and they were not only lookers, having been smartened up with the use of John Cowen's best stuff, the top working and looking stuff that he was breeding before he had his best terriers stolen – stuff that had produced Cowen's famous Rock, a dog that not only won well at shows, but also worked well for the Melbreak foxhounds. Another terrier Barry has used in more recent years was Middleton's Chad, a strong, very good looking terrier with a massive head – a quality that was put into this strain by frequent matings to Wilkinson's Rock. Chad sired Teezer, an ultra-game bitch who has won several shows.

Barry also used a terrier bred by Frank Stacey of the Holme Valley beagles. Stacey bred blacks and Wild used a son of Satan, a dog with a massive head. Some of the heads on Wild's terriers are truly magnificent and stand them in good stead when up to a tough hill fox that won't bolt. Barry believes that Frank Stacey's black stuff was Gould/Middleton bred. Tommy Skidmore had a dog out of Ward's superb looker and worker, Printer, and Wild also used this dog as outcross blood. He also stated that Ward bred some superb black stuff later on, as he said he would, but this seems to have had little impact on black Fell terrier bloodlines of recent years.

Barry did much digging with Dave Roberts, especially around Derbyshire, and he lamented on how times have changed. He can clearly remember digging badgers on the edge of Buxton and other villages, or in a field along the side of main roads, and being left alone to get on with it. Once, while digging a fox out of an earth, a police car pulled up and they were asked if there was anything wrong, for the occupants wondered if one of their dogs had been run over, or something of that nature, they were that close to the road, but when they answered that they had caught a fox, the policemen simply told them to carry on, got back in their car and drove away. Another spot was at some crags above a main road where foxes and badgers were often taken from the rockpiles below these crags. These days, it is impossible to dig in such places as someone would soon be pointing the accusing finger, despite the fact that the digging of foxes (at the time of writing) is perfectly legal and is a necessary means of keeping the fox population under control.

Wild once knew a policeman from Ashton who also used Buck-bred blacks for the digging of foxes and badgers. This terrier was named Hector and was a superb worker, for Barry brought this dog into his strain too. He stated that these terriers, as one would expect from Buck-bred stuff, were superb digging terriers and this was one of the reasons he was glad to bring Hector into his breeding programme.

Barry Wild has a wealth of experience of working terriers to fox and badger (it is now illegal to hunt badgers and so Barry aims to breed fox killers these days) and he has dug with many of the greats, including Bill Brightmore and Dave Roberts, and has

Cassy, bred by Barry Wild: Great Yorkshire Show winner. (Buck/Breay/Middleton).

worked with some superb terriers, some of which are among the most important studs in Fell terrier history, terriers such as Middleton's Rex and Dave Roberts' Rip. He is a good judge of a terrier and knows his stuff. I have appointed him to judge one or two of my own shows in the past and he has done a superb job. He has also judged the Great Yorkshire show during the days when blacks, black and tans and reds were all lumped together in one class. He believes it is much easier these days, now that they have split colours into different categories. It was very hard work, he said, judging classes with huge amounts of terriers of all colours before you. Many accuse Wild of breeding show dogs only, but he is quick to stress that his dogs are still first and fore-most workers. He does not do as much hunting these days, true, with work commitments and one thing or another, but he still works his dogs whenever possible. When he cannot, his son works them in his place and he has had quite a number of foxes using his father's terriers in recent years. So disregard the idea that these black terriers, Patterdales, black Fells, or black Lakelands, call them what you will, from Wild's strain are non-workers. Not all are hard, true, but most will go if given a fair chance. I have a bitch from this strain and she is a wonderful worker, a true finder and a good bolting bitch. She is also useful for digging foxes as she is not too hard and will stand off and bay at her quarry. It is true that there are some who only show, and do not work their terriers, as is the case with some who keep Middleton-bred terriers, but the founder of the strain cannot be blamed for that! Generally speaking, the terriers of Barry Wild's superb looking strain are workers, and good workers at that.

As is the case with Fell terriers, there are two types of Patterdale terrier that are being bred and worked today; the smooth coated black and red terriers and the harder coated type which, in the main, have come from the terriers of Brian Nuttall, stuff that works wonderfully well, but, generally, is not in any way suited to the show ring, and the more typey black terriers which are rough coated and much more suitable for use as show dogs, though many of these also work as well as they look. These have been smartened up with typey unregistered Lakelands such as those bred by Middleton, Ward and Cowen and many do not view them as Patterdales, just like the older generation of fell-hunters do not view the smooth and harsh coated terriers produced by Nuttall as Patterdales. There is much confusion as to what is a Patterdale, but one thing is for certain; all of these terriers, the smooths as well as rough coated types, as well as the typey and untypey strains, have come from the same rootstock: that originally created by Cyril Breay and Frank Buck. It was these terriers which first began being labelled as Patterdales, after this term had fallen into disuse regarding the old strains of Lakeland terrier which were once extensively bred in this area, and so terriers of that same type are now generally known as Patterdales whether they are typey or not. Do not forget, Buck and Breay also produced a lot of typey stuff which won well in the ring, though it is also true to say that much of it would have done very badly at shows.

Although Nuttall never breeds for show, a few very smart terriers do crop up in litters from time to time. Jack Smith's Ranter was bred out of Nuttall stock and this terrier produced Oliver Gill's Beano, one of the most typey terriers ever bred. Brock, owned by Barry and Danny Hill, is out of Nuttall stock, along with a touch of Gould blood, and he is incredibly typey too. Gould's dog Smithy (Blacksmith) was out of a Nuttall bitch and Brian says that Didricksen bred him out of a Cowen stud dog (it was rumoured that Middleton stuff may have been partly respon-sible, but Nuttall is adamant that Didricksen bred this terrier out of a Cowen dog). Smithy produced much better looking black terriers which not only worked well, but won well at shows too. Nuttall currently has a terrier named Buster who is a handsome dog with a magnificent head. He is not a world-beater, but he is smart enough to compete in the show ring.

Danny Sykes and Mark Hallet are two more breeders of typey black stuff, which also works very well indeed. Danny often digs with Dave Mitchell, and his terriers, like all others of this type, originally go back to the dogs of Buck and Breay. Do not forget, this pair of terrier enthusiasts were prolific breeders of superb working stuff and large numbers were literally scattered all over the country. Thanks to breeders such as Ken Gould, Bill Brightmore, Barry Wild, Mark Hallet, John Parkes and Brian Nuttall in particular, what are now so commonly known as Patterdale terriers are a very common type of working terrier which is becoming ever-more popular with each passing year. I would like to have covered other top breeders in far more detail, but there just isn't the room in a book of this size. However, the main breeding of modern Patterdale terriers has been covered thoroughly and it soon becomes obvious what a huge role those early breeders, Buck, Breay, Akerigg, Nuttall, played in the development of Patterdale terriers. Whatever you call them, black Fells, black Lakelands, or Patterdale terriers, one thing is for certain; most of the modern strains are every bit as game as the original bloodlines created by the two 'masters.'

5

PATTERDALES
AND OTHER BREEDS

Do not think that Frank Buck and Cyril Breay bred a 'pure' strain
of what later became known as Patterdale terriers. Brian Nuttall
can remember certain terrier enthusiasts obtaining Cairn and
Scottish terriers from gamekeepers in Scotland and these entered
many strains of working Lakeland, or Fell terriers, producing
shorter legged stock and very often prick-ears in the resultant
offspring. Brian stated that these were not the pedigree dogs of
Scotland, but unregistered working types which were every bit
as game as Fell and Lakeland terriers. It is the same story
throughout the British Isles. Along with the pedigree strains,
there are always one or two working strains left, though many are
now on the edge of extinction. In Scotland, the Patterdale terrier
has become the most popular working breed and few Scottish
terriers, including Cairns etc, are now worked in their native
land.

Nuttall was told by a member of Buck's family that Black
Davey, a wonderful working terrier who also won several
shows, was one quarter bred to a Scottish terrier; one of the
unregistered working strains kept by keepers and some crofters
in order to tackle vermin such as wildcats and foxes, and I can
well believe this, for Davey had two prick-ears which were
dropped by the local vet. Other terriers in the strain developed
one prick-ear and this fault still occurs today. Nuttall is certain
that Scottish-bred working terriers were responsible for introducing this fault into many strains of Fell terriers and that this
fault, which is still evident on many Patterdale and Fell terriers
today, was introduced to the line through Black Davey; the
powerful square head of this terrier also being another indicator
of such a cross.

Buck and Breay also used much Border terrier blood in their

Fell, hunting a huge rockpile in West Yorkshire.

strain and they were no worse off for that. Frank Buck obtained many Border terriers and three-quarter bred Borders from the Zetland and Bedale hunt countries and these entered the strain produced by both Buck and Breay. True, during those early years, they were establishing a strain and all sorts went into the mix, including those game Sealyham terriers which Breay and his father used for badger digging, bringing them to the north from South Wales and crossing them with the gamest of local Fell types. But even after their strain had been well and truly established for many years, they continued to put other blood into the mix, the most obvious being the Border terrier blood of Akerigg's well known bitch, Lasty. She was a three-quarter bred Border, but Middleton stated that if her tail had not been docked she would have passed for a pure Border.

I believe that Buck and Breay turned to Border terrier blood once again in order to calm the fiery nature that had cropped up because of Bull blood being introduced from that black-brindle and white dog which Buck took with him on those digs organised by Mr and Mrs Williams. Many dogs of this strain were just too hard and lacked sense. This would not have pleased Breay, for, although he loved gameness in a terrier, he also aimed for sense below ground, for he was a serious badger digger who took part in this activity right up to his death. In order to produce game, but sensible dogs – an essential quality in a badger digging dog – a cross with the old fashioned Border bloodlines would undoubtedly do the trick, for many fell-hunters of the time were using Border terrier blood to cool down the fiery disposition of Fell strains, which were taking too much punishment while at work. Lasty was bred out of the old fashioned Border, for Middleton believes she was out of the Williams strain; superb workers which acquitted themselves well against all types of quarry, including badger, fox and otter.

As we can see, both Breay and Buck crossed their Patterdale terriers with other breeds in order to get what they wanted, even after their strain had become well and truly established. Many do the same today and are enjoying good results from such practices.

One sees adverts from time to time for Patterdale/Border pups, or Patterdale/Fell pups, but one of the most attractive of all Patterdale crosses is the Jack Russell cross. Many typey black and white, or tri-coloured offspring result from such a cross and many of these are superb workers too. Jack Russells tend to be a little on the yappy side and some can be a little too aggressive. However, putting a Patterdale terrier onto a Russell will do much to calm down this fiery disposition which can make Russells one of the most irritating of terrier breeds to keep. Also, Patterdale terrier blood will improve coat in a Russell dramatically, not to mention working ability, though very often the offspring will be harder than a traditional Jack Russell, which was originally bred to stand off, bay at, and bolt its fox. True, the offspring are generally harder, but still, they usually have enough sense not to get themselves too badly knocked about. If one chooses a strain which has no Bull terrier in its recent past, then one will get terriers which may be fox killers, but without that disposition which means a terrier will grab a fox anywhere and take a serious mauling as a result. Nuttall rates sense very highly as he believes a terrier should be fit for work for two or three days a week during an average season.

When Barry Wild put Middleton's Moss to one of his black bitches, one of the puppies was a black and white bitch. Many of these Russell-marked Fell terriers are used by serious Russell breeders in order to improve general type in their strains. A white Lakeland, or a Patterdale/Russell will usually improve coat type, bone structure and will put better heads into a strain which has

Patterdales played an important part in the development of Plummer Terriers. The author judging at the Midland Game Fair.

become weaker over the years. I am pretty certain that at least ninety-five per cent of the top winning Russells today have white Lakeland in their bloodlines, while a good percentage are full-blown white Lakelands.

Plummer terriers are a very attractive, eye-catching breed of terrier which has grown tremendously in popularity in recent years. There is much controversy over the separate breeding programmes of The Plummer Terrier Association and The Plummer Terrier Club of Great Britain at the time of writing, but it would be out of place to delve into this subject in the pages of this book. The reason for mentioning this relatively new breed of terrier is because Plummer terriers have a good deal of Patterdale terrier blood in their make-up. In order to ascertain why Brian should use such blood, we must first examine his early breeding programme.

I found my discussions with Plummer to be fascinating experiences indeed. He was a very interesting and knowledgeable gentleman and we discussed his breeding programme on more than one occasion. Brian started with small rough and ready terriers, which were used for all kinds of pest control throughout the valleys of South Wales; terriers that may have come from the same rootstock as the Sealyham which Breay and his father took with them to the North of England where they found them to be unsuited to the difficult terrain in and around the Northern Pennines – the same country hunted by Fred Barker during his days as Huntsman to the original Pennine foxhounds.

Plummer found these terriers to be useful, but many lacked good nose and voice was definitely found wanting as many of these earth dogs would not bay when up to their quarry. Hence Brian turned to good working Jack Russell blood in order to improve both nose and voice. Russells were originally bred, in part, out of Beagle blood and this cross has given this breed nose and a very vociferous bay when up to quarry.

The scruffy white terriers from South Wales also had a tendency to be too hard, many of them taking severe maulings while at work. Even when crossed with Russells, some of the offspring remained too hard as Brian was a serious badger digger at the time and quite a number of these dogs suffered badly when engaged in such activities. Plummer then took the advice of an eighteenth century poem, which he was very familiar with. If one has a

> fighting, biting curr, who lyes
> And is scarce heard, but often kills the fox,
> With such a one, bid him a beagle join

advises this ancient poem that was obviously written by someone who knew their subject. Brian did just that. A friend of his owned an American bred Beagle, from pedigree stock of course, but it was small and incredibly game, for it accompanied the terriers on badger digs and proved itself a wonderful finder and stayer, cleverly keeping out of trouble by baying at its foe until dug out. Brian was doing much badger and fox digging at this time and both his terriers and this Beagle were tested to the full. Satisfied that this was the right dog to bring into the strain, Plummer now put the Beagle to his bitches and bred some incredibly useful stock; stock which packed well, found well and also had sense enough to stay out of trouble whilst working badgers – one of the most formidable opponents that any terrier could face.

This stock was ugly though, having large houndy ears. I suppose this was an improvement, on the prick-ears that were so prevalent before Beagle blood was added to the mix. It was this Beagle that first introduced the blanket markings and the fiery red colour one now associates with Plummer terriers. Brian now began fixing type, but he soon had problems with weak heads and other faults such as cleft pallets. In order to correct these and breed them out of his strain, Bull terrier blood was introduced and this did indeed do the trick, though Brian had major problems, as one would expect, with kennel fights. When terriers are keener to latch onto each other, rather than stand against their quarry, then drastic action must be undertaken. When I had a bitch, which was the last terrier in a strain I had begun, I declined to breed from her for this very reason. If I took her out with a lurcher, intending to bolt the fox for the lurcher to course, she would be eager to tackle the lurcher before she went to her fox. Not that she was a poor worker. In fact, her very first time to fox was in a deep mineshaft where she was to ground for well over three hours and she succeeded in bolting two foxes during that time. But bad fighters are pretty nigh-on useless to a terrierman and cannot be tolerated.

In order to improve colour, which had weakened with the introduction of Bull terrier blood, and to calm down the fiery fighting temper, Brian now introduced Patterdale terrier blood from a red dog bred by Nigel Hinchliffe of the Pennine foxhounds; a dog bred out of Breay and Nuttall stock. Pip, a Jack Russell owned by Forsyth, was also put onto Plummer bitches.

Pip was descended from Jim Blake's Breach-bred Jack Russells and had proved an excellent worker, as had the dog bred by Hinchliffe. Even more Patterdale blood was added later on and this did much to calm down the tendency to fight. Patterdale blood also put superb heads and straight, narrow fronts into the breed, qualities which are still much in evidence today. Patterdale terriers also tend to have dense coats, even though smooth, which keep out the wet and cold. The Plummer terrier should still have this dense jacket, rather than a jacket similar to a whippet, which gives much protection from the elements. I have seen Plummer terriers working in awful conditions and they have been unaffected and have got on with their vocation without flinching.

So Brian not only improved temperament with the use of Patterdale blood, but also put hardiness into his breed.

The terriers bred by Plummer were now tested to the full and while scores were put out at hunt service with several packs throughout the Midlands, Brian continued digging many foxes and badgers in and around Derbyshire and Leicestershire in particular. So Plummer terriers are bred from out and out workers that proved themselves hunting a variety of different quarry. Quite a bit of the hunting instinct and the hardiness of this attractive breed of terrier is due to the addition of Patterdale terrier blood, particularly the Patterdales bred by Brian Nuttall of Cheshire.

Patterdales have an instinct for work that is second to none and they are incredibly useful for 'spicing-up' any strain of earth dog that is proving a little inferior. A strain of working terrier can

Brian Nuttall with Buster; note the dog's powerful head!

weaken over the years, for whatever reason, and the inclusion of this blood will do much to improve both hardiness and working ability.

Do not forget, Nuttall has worked his terriers throughout the length and breadth of the British Isles and they have proven themselves incredibly useful earth dogs with a variety of different packs, from fell packs to shire packs, and so one can be assured that this type of terrier has been tested to the full. Brian may not kill a lot of foxes, but he still requires his terriers to both find and stay until dug out. Some of his terriers are fox killers too, but they are sensible in the main, though, as Barry Wild stated, some of them are just too hard. One would expect this from a type of dog which, in part, is descended from Bull terrier stock, both from his grandfather's strain, and the dogs of Buck and Breay.

Patterdale terriers have had a massive impact on the world of the working terrier during recent years and this is down to the breeding programmes of enthusiasts such as Parkes, Nuttall and, more recently, professional terriermen such as Dave Finlay and Nick Stevens. Many do find them too hard for what they require in a working terrier and thus Patterdales, admired for their sheer guts and determination, have been used, as we have seen, as outcross blood for many strains and as a cross with other breeds such as Jack Russells and Lakelands. The working instinct of any strain of terrier can quickly be improved with a little addition of Patterdale terrier blood.

6

THE VERSATILE
PATTERDALE

During those days when Cyril Breay and Frank Buck were at the height of their success with breeding their own strain that eventually became known as the Patterdale terrier, badger digging was still a legal country pursuit which, in rural areas anyway, was also considered respectable as a means of carrying out pest control. This activity was carried out in a humane manner and most of the badgers taken were released elsewhere, usually into areas where badgers were noticeable by their absence, though many were dug out and shot at the request of the landowner.

While it is true to say that Buck/Breay bred terriers have proven useful for this activity in the main, it is also a fact that many were just too hard for tackling badgers deep in their sett where they can easily outwit all but the gamest and most determined of terriers. Legion are the tales of earth dogs which went to ground on Brock and emerged half an hour or so later, thoroughly beaten and sometimes with pieces of their jaw missing. If the diggers had got two or three feet down by this time, it would have been the most irritating and frustrating thing in the world for them to have their terrier come off its quarry. True, another could be quickly entered, but Brock would undoubtedly have moved on by the time another dog found and so digging operations would need to begin again. Also, the injured terrier would have to be taken home, or at least to the nearest farm, for treatment and that would mean being a man down. So the hard terrier, the 'won't give an inch' sort of temperament, was nigh-on useless to the serious badger digger who would need to succeed in his endeavours if he was going to be invited onto a farm, or onto keepered land, again.

Many of the Patterdale terriers being bred in those far off days,

Patterdale terriers belonging to Brian Nuttall.

though extremely game, were just not sensible enough for the activity of digging out badgers which tested the courage of any terrier to the ultimate limit. And so, severe injuries, even death, were the result of even a short period of time to ground on these belligerent animals. Remember, badgers are simply very large ferrets and they can strike with incredible swiftness and with a bite that would make a bear trap look like a child's toy. Thus hard terriers suffered very badly when engaged in such earthwork.

Nuttall says that a badger-digging terrier had to stand its ground when Brock charged, but that it must do so in a way which left it uninjured. If a terrier stood head-on to a badger, the results were often horrendous, but a clever dog would dodge the oncoming attack and would seize Brock by the cheek, thus preventing it from getting past and quickly sending it back to the stop end. When Brock turned around in order to dig on, the clever terrier would then seize it by the back end, forcing it to turn around once more and thus keeping it occupied. A badger would sit in the hole-end at times without moving while its opponent bayed continuously. After a while though, the quarry would charge with a burst of anger and the terrier would then employ those clever tactics once more in order to keep its foe in the stop-end of the sett, having to do so until the diggers arrived.

This could take hours of strenuous effort by a team of diggers and a terrier must stay during that time. If the earth dog emerged to take a breather for a few minutes, then Brock would be on the move in that time and, again, a lot of effort would have been wasted. True, young terriers just learning their trade would occasionally emerge for air, even during fox digs this can happen, but they will very quickly grow out of this as they become more experienced and will learn to stay until reached – if they are made of the right stuff that is. Some would then use a seizure dog at the end of digs, such as a Bull terrier, which would grab the badger by the cheek and drag it out so that it could be tailed and placed in a sack for release elsewhere. Barry Wild said that most badger diggers had such dogs at one time, but it is also true that many terriers could both stay during a dig and then seize their quarry at the end of it so that their master could handle the quarry without fear of getting bitten. This ability usually came with experience, but it was borne of a natural instinct which man has taken advantage of for centuries, though no doubt a long line of badger digging dogs would pass on this ability, in some measure, with each new generation of working dog.

This ability to seize their quarry at the end of a dig was highly prized by terriermen who were serious badger diggers, but it was easy enough to draw out this knack of holding quarry at the end of a successful dig. Dogs are naturally jealous and the action of the master uncovering the quarry and moving towards it was enough to make the terrier go for a hold. Naturally, a sensible dog would grab onto an area which meant that it could not be bitten in return, but the dog was simply attempting to claim the prize for itself, not acting in a way that meant its owner would be protected whilst tailing the beast. Once the terrier realised that this action pleased its master and that rewards and praise resulted, the action would be reinforced and the behaviour would then become a natural pattern.

Gary Middleton tells a fascinating tale of a badger dig that took place on a fellside in the Lake District. He had been asked by a local shepherd to move some badgers, for these creatures do attack and carry off lambs as they are predators and are easily capable of carrying out such activities, especially in areas where food can be scarce. Middleton was an ethusiastic badger digger and shifted hundreds for local farmers. Like many Patterdale, Fell and Lakeland terriers, Gary also bred many dogs that were just too hard for this game. They were natural fox killers and dealt with many such creatures, which refused to bolt from earths, but they tackled Brock in the same manner as they would a fox and the results can easily be imagined. However, many of Middleton's terriers learned to handle their badger with much more sense than others, particularly the bitches, though a few of the dogs also proved useful for this activity too.

Gary and his team of diggers had succeeded in breaking through to their quarry and two badgers had been bottled-up by the terrier. When Middleton asked for the sack in order to secure their quarry while it was transported to the place of release, they suddenly realised that this essential piece of equipment had been overlooked and had been left behind. They racked their brains for a solution to the problem and one would have been to dispatch their quarry and have done with it, but that was not an option, for the landowner wished for them to be released elsewhere. Complying with these wishes, one of the diggers took off his oilskin trousers and a badger was stuffed down each leg, after the bottoms had been tied up with string.

The bulging oilskins were now thrown over Middleton's shoulder and off they went towards their vehicle in the valley bottom, heading for a pre-selected place of release – usually a long disused sett in an area where badgers were no longer found. On the way down the fell Middleton felt the temporary sack become much lighter. On turning round he saw two badgers making off back up the fell towards their sett. If he let them get to ground once more, then the farmer would probably never have him on his land again, so two terriers were released and they went after their fleeing quarry, grabbed the pair of badgers and held them until help arrived shortly afterwards. The string had slipped off the bottom of the legs and the two 'Brocks' had simply slipped out the other end and were off, making a bid for freedom. The ends of the trouser legs were properly secured this time and a successful release took place. Disregard the tales of cruelty and baiting; the true digger always dealt with badgers in a humane manner and most were released elsewhere. Those that were dispatched at the request of the landowner were killed instantly, not tortured by setting large numbers of dogs on them.

Of course, badger digging and the disturbing of a badger sett are now illegal and must be avoided by all terriermen. Patterdales are no longer considered as a viable option as a badger digging terrier, but still, they are incredibly useful for other activities that are legal (I have to put 'at the time of writing' as there is much opposition to all forms of hunting with dogs at the moment, in England and Wales in particular).

Ratting has got to be one of the most exciting and most satisfying of all country pursuits, for one knows that a great service is being done to keepers, farmers and the public in general in ridding the land of these disease-ridden pests. Of course, the hunting man should never aim to eliminate these animals, despite the deadly diseases they carry, but it is essential that their numbers be kept down to a minimum.

Rats are found in large numbers on tips, keepered estates and farms in particular, though they can also be found along canals, rivers and even narrow streams. Particularly in crop-growing areas they can readily be found along hedgerows and drainage dykes surrounding these fields. I have even shifted rats from hunt kennels where the scores of hounds and terriers did nothing to put these cheeky creatures off their task of scrounging as much illegally taken food as possible. Rats, in fact, will live almost anywhere and the most effective method, after poisoning that is, of controlling their numbers is by using terriers. These small dogs have a long association with the hunting of rats and they are ideally equipped for such purposes.

The Patterdale terrier makes a great rat-hunting dog as they have superb noses, an eager interest in finding huntable quarry and enough tenacity to make great rat-killing dogs. The nose has been bred into this strain from earth dogs that have been required to bolt and kill foxes in some of the deepest earths in the country. Both Breay and Buck worked the dreaded earths of the Lake District and North Yorkshire and their dogs had a wide range of deep lairs to tackle; earths such as old mineworkings, huge piles of rock in old quarries, deep and dangerous limestone fissures and vast borrans. Dug-out rabbit holes were tackled too. Especially by Buck who served as terrierman for hunts such as the Bedale and West of Yore who hunt a more gentle country than either the Dales, or the Lake District, but in the main these dogs had to face their work in some incredibly deep and difficult places, places which meant that finding ability was essential. That quality is just as essential today.

Rats will often live among filth. Coupled with farmyard scents and all manner of foul-smelling stuff to be found on tips, one can easily see how good nose is vital if a terrier is to find its quarry

A well-used rat warren.

and mark it to ground. Much time can be wasted in ferreting empty holes, so a dog who will quickly let its master know that 'ratty' is at home is worth its weight in gold. Patterdales have good enough noses to be able to learn this ability to mark very quickly indeed. By simply allowing a terrier to run free, a rat hole will soon be discovered and the dog will quickly let you know if anyone is at home. A dog staring into a hole and wagging its tail furiously, is a sure sign of occupation, as is a terrier digging at the entrance, though one must be quick to stop this digging, lest your terrier block the hole. This ability to mark may be picked up after a few outings, even one or two, but some will have this ability right from day one.

Turk, one of the pups I recently bred, began marking rats from the very first day he was taken out, and marking true at that. Mist, the dam of Turk, a bitch bred out of Barry Wild's black stuff, not only marked rats from the very first day of hunting them, but also did the same with foxes. From day one, she has marked fox earths accurately as to whether they were occupied or not, thus saving huge amounts of time, for much time is consumed whilst waiting for a terrier to explore the dark passages of every earth one comes across. It seems that Mist has passed on this ability to her youngsters.

Patterdales are hard, determined workers and it would be so easy to think that one can start such a terrier at rats early on, but the truth is that the principles of entering apply to Patterdales just as much as they do to any other breed. In fact, in many cases, more so, for there is quite a lot of Border terrier blood in Patterdale strains and so many are really quite sensitive and can so easily be put off their work if entered at too young an age.

Many decry the hunting of rats as a very minor activity that is easily within the capabilities of any terrier, scoffing at the idea that a rat can bite savagely and so put a dog off hunting them. Those same people are usually terrified of rats and will not go near them, for fear of being bitten. Why, if rats are such teeny little weaklings that are unworthy as quarry for working terriers? The truth is, rats do bite with great force, slicing into the skin on a terrier's face. These wounds often bleed profusely, but this is desireable, for it washes out any muck that gets into the wound. Thankfully, after a clean with salt water, these wounds heal very quickly and usually without causing any problems, as long as the dog has been innoculated against Weil's disease (Leptospirosis). Even the hardiest of Patterdales will be dead in a very short time if it is not vaccinated against this deadly rat disease.

I always wait until a terrier is eight months of age before starting it on rats. Some will get stuck into their quarry like veterans at this age, while others will drop their quarry when bitten and allow another dog to grab it before going in again. These will mature in a very short time, once they have joined in killing a few rats, and will soon have the confidence to tackle even the largest of rats on their own. Individual dogs mature at different times and while one may tackle rats eagerly at eight months, another will not. Patience is the watchword in such a situation, for something will click eventually and the slower starter will soon catch up with its more forward companions. As long as you do not enter too early, any breed of terrier will be useful for the hunting of rats, though the sheer pluck and deter-mination of breeds such as Lakelands and Patterdales makes them ideal as ratters.

The best way for a terrier to kill a rat is to shake it whilst biting at the same time. This action usually prevents a rat from biting in return, but not always, for some rats will latch onto a terrier as soon as it is picked up. Other terriers, particularly Patterdales and Lakeland, or Fell terriers, will simply deal with their quarry with a crushing bite, though the chances of themselves being bitten in return are far higher using this method. However, pain seems to drive these breeds onto greater effort and such bites are taken in their stride.

Plummer terriers are renowned rat killing dogs which have made quite a name for themselves at this game, thanks mainly to Brian Plummer who used these dogs extensively for the killing of these rodents, particularly during his time spent in the Midlands where he killed thousands of the beasts with his pack of terriers. When a breed is used extensively for a certain task, something emerges in the genetics of such dogs and this is passed on to the offspring. I believe this has happened with the Plummer terrier, just as something has been passed on in the genetics of Fell terriers which make them superior workers of deep rockpiles and borrans; a characteristic undoubtedly picked up after several decades of working their native landscape.

Long before Nuttall told me of working Cairn and Scottish terriers being brought to the Lakes and entering the bloodlines of native terriers, I believed that dogs from Scotland had gone into the mix as the Scottish breeds in particular had a knack of working some of the deadliest rock earths in the Highlands. These vast borrans, known as cairns north of the border, make the Lake District borrans look like a small heap of pebbles, and the dogs used in such places were something very special indeed. The old Scottish strains were the gamest in the world and I am certain that the Cumbrian strains of terrier inherited this knack for working rock from such ancestors; ancestors which were bred to kill foxes deep in their lairs, if they refused to bolt as those cairns could not possibly be dug. When Nuttall was younger, more Scottish blood entered these strains and their influence can clearly be seen in the shorter legged, prick-eared terriers that still crop up in Fell litters. Nuttall is one hundred per cent certain that Scottish terrier blood (the unregistered strains used by keepers and crofters until recently) went into the Buck/Breay breeding programme and that this produced the powerful square heads on terriers such as Black Davey and, of course, the prick-ears that are still found on dogs of this strain today. Blood from such a cross

Plummer terriers on North Uist; the Patterdale influence has bred hardiness into this breed.

would also reinforce the black colouring, which first appeared in the Buck/Breay strain in 1936.

I believe that Patterdale terrier blood, and Brian certainly used quite a few top working Patterdales on his bitches, has given the Plummer terrier that extra edge which makes them ideal ratting dogs, for there are no more determined workers than Patterdale terriers.

Patterdales have true noses, plenty of guts and determination and agility, one of the more important qualities needed on a ratting dog, for rats are incredibly nimble and are very difficult to catch. When I accompanied Derek Webster to a keepered spot in Cheshire in order to shift rats after the shooting season was over, we worked the warrens that had been dug among the winter crops. Rats will move out of the hedgerows and into the fields, or in any other area, where pheasants are being fed in order to keep them in places to be shot over. Alongside the pheasants rats will feed with much more enthusiasm and large numbers will inhabit these areas, digging vast warrens among the crops. Ferreting these warrens is a good way of bolting the occupants, but there is another very quick way of getting them on the move, a way that I saw for the first time that day.

I have dug rats out of their lairs on several occasions, but usually from riverbanks, or along narrow brooks, even on tips where the lairs can be quite deep. In crop growing areas the warrens are often quite shallow and all one has to do is slice a spade into the earth all around the area of the warren and rats will start bolting very soon after, if one is hitting the right spot and slicing into the tunnels that is. This method is far quicker than digging out a warren and is obviously far less messy. We

Frank Buck with Tex; a terrier with which Frank took hundreds of foxes. Note the white patch on his leg, a common 'fault' with Buck/Breay-bred terriers that I believe came about after Bull terrier blood was introduced into the strain!

stationed ourselves in likely places, but even so, quite a number of rats managed to get past the dogs and out among the crops where they were incredibly difficult to see. Many were caught after much determined effort by my four terriers, with Derek's lurcher, Rocky, a superb all-rounder, catching one or two, but a few made good their escape.

This is why a terrier must be agile. A large bulky dog with much Bull blood in its pedigree is going to be very limited when it comes to the hunting of 'Ratty', for a dog of this build just cannot lunge into the narrowest of gaps, or dodge around farm machinery and all kinds of other obstacles in order to catch a fleeing rodent. The bottoms of hedges are a favourite haunt of 'Ratty' and these are incredibly difficult places from which to hunt rat successfully. For a dog to chase its quarry along a hedge bottom, bobbing and weaving through a great variety of undergrowth, it must be agile. Patterdale terriers are one of the most natural and free moving types of terrier that I have ever seen in action and they are ideal for this task.

The good noses and agility of Patterdales also make them excellent bushing and ferreting dogs. Frank Buck did quite a bit of ferreting with his terriers and Max, his son, remarked that Frank was a superb shot when it came to fast-bolting rabbits. Some of his best workers to fox and badger were also excellent rabbiting dogs and Tex, possibly his most famous terrier, was one of the best ferreting dogs he owned. However, if one will be using terriers in conjunction with hounds, then it is best not to enter to rabbit at all, for one could so easily be shown-up in front of the whole field by a terrier switching from fox to rabbit.

Patterdales are extremely useful for mink-hunting too and Nuttall has used them quite a bit in this capacity, alongside minkhounds, though he rarely hunts these creatures nowadays. A terrier must be very game if it is going to tackle mink, for, not only do they bite with extreme savagery and power, a power well out of proportion to their size, but they also stink to high heaven. Max Buck was telling me of a mink he had killed with one of his young terriers, a bitch named Grip, during the evening before I went up to Leyburn to interview him, and of how he had to drive home with the windows wound right down, the mink stunk that much. Just because of the smell alone, a body scent made far worse by a fish diet, a terrier must be game for anything when it comes to the hunting of such creatures.

Above all things, it is as a hunter of foxes that the Patterdale terrier comes into its own. Frank Buck and Cyril Breay (the creators of the black and red terriers now known as Patterdales, and all black stuff today, along with red and chocolate slape-coated terriers, can be traced back to their strain), along with many of the older generation of fell-hunters, required a terrier to finish a fox below ground if it refused to bolt, for both of them lived in the uplands of Cumbria and North Yorkshire where foxes can take many lambs and poultry such as chickens. Farmers require a fox to be accounted for in such circumstances and the terrierman who makes all sorts of excuses for not getting their fox would be chased off the land and shot if he ever stepped onto the place again! Baying terriers are not suitable in such areas when lambs and poultry are taken, for Reynard often knows the un-diggable spots and will very often not bolt from such fortresses. Hence the reason for breeding dogs that were capable of killing a fox in a tussle deep underground.

Nuttall says that Buck started in terriers when Cyril Breay gave him his first dog, a bitch named Tickler, but my research leads me to question this. Max Buck told me that Frank often talked about his time growing up in the village where his father dealt in horses, carrying on the tradition from his father before him, and of his times spent rabbiting with a terrier and a ferret in the countryside around Appersett (the village where Frank was born and raised)

Brick, a superb worker. Owned by Danny Sykes.

and Hawes. And so Frank Buck was already well acquainted with terriers long before he met Mr Breay. However, Nuttall is correct in part, for I believe that it was Breay who kindled Buck's interest in working foxes on a regular basis, for prior to this he would put a terrier in a game bag, which he carried over his shoulders, and ride around the Yorkshire countryside on an ancient motorcycle in search of rabbits and other game suitable for the pot.

He used to work for his father, helping out with the horses and riding for him at shows and competitions where horses were trotted, rather than galloped, but was finished when he left home to get married and start a family. Buck's father told him he would get nothing if he left home and that is exactly what happened. Now in need of work, Frank went to the racing stables at Middleham and was employed to help exercise and look after the valuable animals kept there. Shortly afterwards, he took up employment as a wagon driver. It was during this time that Frank met Breay and the unusual partnership, a partnership that was to last right up until Breay died, began, with the aim of breeding some of the gamest and most useful terriers in the world.

It was also at this time that Frank began doing the part-time terrier work for the Bedale foxhounds and his terriers proved most useful and earned him a reputation second to none in a relatively short time, though he also did much private hunting in those days and shifted foxes for gamekeepers and farmers alike, very often after they had lost lambs and poultry to these predators. In fact, it wasn't long before Buck was in great demand throughout the Dales, and beyond.

Whilst interviewing Max Buck, Frank's eldest son, he showed me many old photographs and newspaper clippings concerning the dogs and exploits of his father. One of these news stories was concerning fox predation throughout the Wensleydale area many years ago. After one hundred lambs and over four hundred chickens had been taken by marauding foxes from farms scattered throughout this region, a committee was set up and people called in to deal with the problem. Frank Buck did by far the majority of this work and was paid a bounty for each fox he caught. Along with the efforts of one or two others, this group of hunters accounted for 216 foxes in just one year. Frank dug foxes in those days, as he did throughout his long and eventful life, and quite a few were killed below by his terriers, but the majority were bolted and shot. Max says his father was a very good shot and he usually brought a fox down with just one barrel. Max also confirmed what Roger Westmoreland had told me earlier – that Frank treated his quarry in a humane manner, always killing it with a single shot as soon as the animal was dug out, or bolted; an admirable approach and one well worth imitating today!

Frank's father-in-law, a man called Robinson, had at one time been the Huntsman of the original Wensleydale harriers and Frank wanted to revive the pack. He had changed his job by this time and was now driving a milk-tanker for a local dairy, a job that meant he was out driving all night, but now he had much time to spare during the daylight and pursued his goal of reviving the Harrier pack. Donald Sinclair (better known as Siegfried Farnon in the books by James Herriot) and Frank Buck eventually got this pack started again and Sinclair was the Master and Huntsman, though Frank hunted the pack during the times that Sinclair, who was, after all, a busy vet, could not make it. While Sinclair hunted on horseback, Buck was a foot-Huntsman. In the old days this method was used very much by harrier packs, including the Holcombe hunt – the oldest harrier pack in the country.

Max stated that his father would go to work all night and then, upon arriving home in the morning, would go down to the kennels near his home at Harmby (a small village near Leyburn and part of the Leyburn district) and see to his hounds first, before going back to his house for breakfast and, if possible, an hour or two of much-needed sleep. And then, after a quick nap, he would be out hunting, either with hounds, or shifting troublesome predators for keepers and farmers. Buck must have been a hyper-active hunter in those days, for most days would see him out with his hounds and terriers in pursuit of the fox. He dug many badgers too, but was mainly a fox-hunting man.

Frank hunted the Wensleydale harriers under the mastership of Donald Sinclair for many years and both foxes and hares were pursued by this pack. Although set up mainly to hunt hares, the local farmers suffered so many problems that Frank and Donald were often asked to hunt foxes instead, sometimes having to go to specific places in order to deal with rogue hill foxes, many of which were accounted for on hunting days.

Frank Buck and Donald Sinclair were great friends and it seems likely that they met at one of the stables where Frank rode out on the racehorses, for Sinclair, as one gathers from James Herriot's superb books, was a specialist horse vet who treated the animals of many stables at one time, particularly throughout Coverdale.

Donald Sinclair (Siegfreid Farnon of James Herriot's books) heading for the first draw with the Wensleydale harriers. Donald and Frank were great friends.

Sinclair also treated Buck's terriers free of charge and must have saved him a fortune on vet's fees.

It must have been a hard life, however, for Frank, working all night and then coming home to many couples of hounds and several terriers to see to, but at least he had the assistance of his family. Max grew up with hounds and terriers and often helped to look after the harriers. He has not so fond memories of springtime at the kennels when he would spend hours collecting and skinning dead sheep and lambs. One spring they were so overrun with lamb carcasses that they had to get in touch with a family friend, John Bulman who hunted the Windermere harriers at that time, in order for him to take some off their hands. Max would put the carcasses in a tin shed where they dried out in no time and lasted for a good while until hounds could munch their way through the grisly foodstocks.

When he had finished hunting the Wensleydale harriers and they were disbanded once more, Frank once again became terrier-man for a pack of hounds – the West of Yore. He held this post for many years, through three masterships in fact, and Max has a mounted fox head on his wall, which his father dug with the terriers while out with this pack. However, Buck could now only hunt part-time because of the dairy closing down, for he now began driving wagons for a local quarry and so worked during the day for many years, until, at last, he retired and could do terrier work full-time once again.

After Max had left home and had settled in order to start a family of his own, he and his father bred and gave each other dogs, but all of Buck junior's stock was from the original Buck/Breay breeding programme and the vast majority were superb workers. Max was a young lad when Tex was on the scene and he often exercised the dog for his father. One day Max and a friend of his were out walking this famous terrier near Harmby when he entered a hole under a tree; a difficult uphill earth where a fox can easily 'boss' a terrier. Tex was made of stern stuff, however, and he soon began baying furiously. After some time, the fox backed out to the bolt-hole and Tex killed it there. Max states that there were far more foxes around back then in the Dales. He believes the lower numbers today are due to fox calling to guns on the lamp. At one time, all keepers would call in hounds, or hunters such as Frank Buck to deal with the local fox population, but nowadays many are dealing with them by using calls to draw them into the lamp and thus within range. This can be a most effective way of dealing with foxes, but sometimes it is too effective and the fox population can be decimated, rather than kept at a healthy level. Hunting with hounds and terriers is far more selective and tends to maintain a healthy number of foxes; neither too few, nor too many.

One of the terriers Frank gave to his son was Adder, an excellent worker with two prick-ears. Max sold this terrier to Wales where it suffocated in a sand hole. Frank also had terriers from his son's breeding and one of the most important matings in the Buck/Breay breeding programme was actually instigated by Max Buck. He owned a chocolate bitch at the time named Tina and he took her to be mated to Harry Hardasty's famous terrier, Turk, a looker, but also an excellent worker who served for many seasons with the Melbreak hunt. Out of this union came Daz, a very important bitch who, like her sire, was very typey indeed, though she was also a wonderful working bitch. Roger Westmoreland's Biddie was from the same litter that produced Daz.

I believe that much of the later stuff Frank Buck was winning with at all of the top shows, including the Great Yorkshire show which he won on at least two occasions, was descended from this important brood bitch. Certainly, all of Max's stuff can be traced back to Daz and he bred Flint from this line, a terrier with which Frank won the Great Yorkshire show in 1987. I was there that year and wanted to approach Buck, but I never summoned the courage to do so. I have many regrets that I never met Frank, except for seeing him at shows, for he had an amazing memory and the information for this book would have been far more detailed had I done so.

Flint, the Yorkshire show winner who was also a wonderful worker, was mated to Walker's bitch, a terrier from the Buck/Breay breeding, and this union produced Ike and Joe, two extremely game workers to fox. Ike proved too game. He saw much service with the West of Yore, but had to be put down after a severe mauling. Joe was returned to Max after the chap who had him suddenly gave up terrier work, and was passed onto his father who sold him. Max wasn't too pleased about this, for Joe was a first class worker, but he laughed philosophically, for, as John Parkes has stated, with Frank 'every dog had its price'.

Max bred in small numbers and produced some excellent stuff. Daz was a very game bitch and he believes that Ike was probably the best worker he has ever bred. Frank, however, bred in very large batches and sent his stock all over the country and abroad. Ireland has had quite a large influx of Frank's terriers and Max is certain he sent quite a number over to America too. And so he was constantly breeding first class workers and that is why he could sell even one of his best terriers. Middleton is the same. For him, the challenge of continuing to produce good looking and good working stock is the reason he breeds terriers and that is why he sells on so many of his top winning and top working stuff – in order to make room for young stock, which he delights in entering and showing. Middleton shows to win and the consistency of producing top winning stuff is what gives him a buzz.

As one would expect, Max hunted with his father on many occasions and he accompanied Frank and Cyril Breay on many trips to keepered spots around Thirsk where they carried out much fox control. Breay often brought a rough haired bitch, a bitch that Max believes had quite a bit of Bedlington in its bloodlines, on these outings to Thirsk and other keepered estates. She was named Kitty and was a first class bitch to ground. At one place near Leeming, they found an earth under a chicken shed and Breay entered Kitty. The farmer had been losing livestock and so they began digging to the bitch who had now found, keen to account for any foxes in the area. When they got down to her, Kitty had bottled up a litter of cubs. Max was quick to stress that these were by now well-grown cubs and they were obviously taking the easy option and eating the occupants of the pen where they had made their home. Max hunted with several of Breay's terriers and he remembers them as being very good working stock.

Max has the hard work of Cyril Breay and Frank Buck, his

Twig and Chris: two terriers bred by Frank Buck.

father, to thank for the stock he continues to keep to this day, though, as I have stated, he has also played quite an important part in this breeding programme too, particularly from the late fifties onwards. At Thirsk, on another keepered estate, Max entered his bitch, Candy, into an earth and they netted the bolt-holes. It wasn't long before she began baying and ten minutes later a fox hit the net. Max, like his father, deals with his quarry humanely and finished the fox instantly with the humane killer. After re-setting the net, Candy now being at yet another fox, he stood back and ten minutes later a second fox hit the net and was swiftly dealt with.

The bitch failed to appear and Max soon heard her at a third fox. This one, however, stood its ground and so they began digging down to the bitch. They soon reached her and dispatched this fox too – a third vixen which, like the other two, was in cub. Would all three vixens have had their cubs in that one earth? I wonder. Brian Plummer, in *The Fell Terrier*, tells of vixens sharing breeding earths up in the fells, but this was among the lowland pastures and woodlands around Thirsk and would have been an unheard of event, if they had shared that same earth. As it was, three vixens in cub were removed and lots of game and farm live-stock would have been saved on that day.

At another spot, a terrier was put to ground and a fox quickly bolted into the net, a vixen which, typically, was quickly dealt with. Max then saw a cub pop its head out and go back. Having a young terrier with him, he decided to loose it, for a first dig on cubs can do much to build the confidence of a youngster. The trouble was, another vixen was also in the earth and Max feared that he had over-faced his young entry. They dug as quickly as possible and eventually uncovered a vixen and cubs. Mist, the young bitch, was unharmed by the encounter, but Max couldn't believe what they found inside that earth. Piles and piles of dead piglets were everywhere, which had obviously been taken from the nearby piggery and carried to the breeding den by the vixen. There were literally scores of them and far too many to be consumed. As I stated earlier in the book, the killing of cubs, or vixens in cub, is totally unacceptable, unless, of course, in circum-stances such as this when livestock is being taken. It is the same with chickens and lambs. Far more are killed than are actually eaten and such activities must be stopped, for a man's livelihood is at stake. This was the one and only time that he has seen another vixen helping in the rearing of another vixen's family.

Candy, the bitch mentioned earlier, once bolted four foxes from the same earth while out with the West of Yore. He said she was a very good working bitch and quite a looker too, but she was too fond of rabbits and was constantly disappearing down rabbit holes, so, in the end, he gave her away. A dog which is over-keen on bunny is of little use to anyone who works their terriers in conjunction with hounds.

Max has only ever been embarrassed on just the one occasion while out with hounds. His terriers have never let him down when hounds have run a fox to ground, or marked an earth, but his little bitch, Grip, a prick-eared sort, a bitch who is of a handy size, for, as Max stated, 'she can get anywhere', recently made his toes curl while out with the West of Yore. Hounds were marking an earth extremely keenly and Max decided to enter Grip. She flew to ground eagerly, but quickly emerged with a rat in her mouth. The place proved to be overrun with rats and no fox was at home, understandably. He was embarrassed, but it was really the hounds' fault for marking rats in the first place.

Max has the head of a fox in his hallway that was caught in 1961 by the Lunesdale foxhounds. Walt Parkin was Huntsman then and both Buck senior and Buck junior hunted with this pack, along with Cyril Breay of course. In fact, Frank was a very close friend of Parkin's and the pair certainly interchanged dogs. It says something of the abilities of Parkin's earth dogs that Buck and Breay brought this blood into their own strain, for Walter was one of the colourful band of Huntsmen who were just as keen on breeding top working terriers as they were on producing top quality hounds.

A fox was found on that morning and was quickly run to ground. A terrier was entered and the fox bolted, but, a few minutes later, went to ground again. Once more, a terrier was 'put in' and Reynard was evicted for a second time. Reluctant to run, the fox went to earth for a third time and was yet again bolted by a terrier. Max recalls that Walter Parkin's dogs were used on this occasion. After another short run, Reynard 'binked' on a ledge at a steep and dangerous crag. Max can remember being on hands and knees and peering nervously over the edge of this sheer drop, while Parkin stood there with his boots partly overhanging the rock edge and looking down on the fox without a care in the world.

Hounds couldn't follow their quarry and so stones were thrown in order to shift it. Foxes can often be given best when at a difficult spot in the shires, but not so in the fells. Every effort is made to account for a fox for the sake of the farmers and so they continued to attempt to move Reynard who was more than a little reluctant to run. At last, they succeeded in shifting him and hounds caught him soon after. The writing on the plaque says that he weighed seventeen pounds; an average weight for a hill fox.

During the war Frank became firm friends with a Canadian soldier who was stationed at Leeming. His name was Al and he often accompanied Frank Buck when he went fox-hunting, helping to keep the fox population down to a minimum for the farmers of the Dales, for, with hunting of hounds suspended, fox numbers would increase dramatically during the war years. Frank often told of one time when Frank took Al along on a hunt over Pennhill near Leyburn, a place where Buck hunted on many occasions over the years, usually clearing foxes for local keepers.

Buck shot a lot of foxes in those days, after bolting them with terriers, and he was using this tried and tested method on this particular day. A terrier was entered into one of the many rocky laybrinths on Pennhill and soon after a fox was bolted. Al then pulled a machine gun out from under his jacket and began shooting at the fleeing beast, much to Frank's amazement.

Now Frank Buck was what you would call a 'tourist baiter', that is, he would tell all manner of tall tales to people in pubs, or those who travelled up to the Dales for a puppy etc. So one may question the authenticity of this story. However, although Max knew of the mischief his father could get up to, he stated that Frank often repeated this tale, even to his own family, and so he is absolutely certain that it is true.

Regarding this tourist baiting, Wendy Pinkney told me an interesting tale of how Frank began spinning yarns when some lads travelled up to his house in order to book a puppy. Max says that their home at Harmby was an open house and visitors were almost constant, so Frank had plenty of 'victims' to go at. A bitch of his was being lined at the time and she had recently been working a fox. Her head was swollen with the bites and Frank told his would-be customers that, because the head of his bitch was swollen at the time of the mating, the puppies would all come with massive, strong heads. They went away eagerly awaiting the arrival of their pups which would have huge, powerful heads that would stand them in good stead when up to a fox! Frank told many similar yarns to his visitors and Dales tourists alike.

Although Patterdale terriers make superb fox dogs and hunt terriers in particular, sometimes they become trapped below ground after either killing their fox, or bolting it. There are bad places countrywide, but the Dales has some of the worst and so Frank was called out on numerous occasions in order to help rescue trapped terriers, very often those of his own strain which had been sold to keepers, hunt terriermen and those who carried out fox control privately. Bill Lambert, a gamekeeper, was one of those who kept Frank's dogs (very few didn't) and his terrier, a small rough haired type, was rescued by Frank and the report appeared in the *Yorkshire Post* and the *Yorkshire Evening Post*. In fact, the vast majority of his rescues and many of his hunts with the Wensleydale harriers were reported in newspapers, for a journalist who lived at Leyburn 'would follow Frank everywhere, taking photographs and jotting down notes', said Max.

Frank told Max that Bill Lambert was an extraordinarily good shot, particularly when shooting bolting foxes. He was out one day with three other guns and a fox was bolted by one of Frank's terriers, for Buck was doing the terrier work for the gamekeeper. The other three guns all had a shot, one after the other, at the fleeing fox and all missed, not even peppering the beast. Lambert shouted 'asta finished' to the party of red-faced guns and then took down the fox with a single shot. Foxes can make very difficult targets when bolting from an earth and they can be so easily missed, but Bill Lambert, and, indeed, Frank Buck himself, missed very few.

One of the best shots I have ever seen was on a keepered estate in Cheshire. We had spent all morning going around the earths and trying them, but each time Fell would tell us that nothing was at home. On almost the last earth we visited, Derek Webster's lurcher marked and Fell confirmed this as being occupied. Once we were all in place, I loosed Fell and he shot into the earth. It was very tight in places and I could hear him digging on, but it wasn't long before he had negotiated this large earth and at last found his fox, the furious baying interrupting the silence of the morning. A fox came out of that earth like a bullet from a gun and the Headkeeper raised his shotgun, took aim and fired, bringing that fox down and killing it instantly. Bolting foxes to waiting guns must be one of the most humane ways of dealing with problem foxes and this was a method Frank Buck used often.

Frank was called in by a farmer after seven lambs had been taken from his fields. Buck found the breeding earth in rocks half a mile from Addlebrough, the flat-topped fell in Wensleydale. Tex and Chew were entered and four cubs were quickly taken by the two terriers, before they turned their attention to the vixen which they soon found and killed. Once the struggle was over, however, the two terriers fell thirty feet down a crevice and a rescue was needed if they were going to be recovered alive.

Digging operations commenced at 9 am and continued throughout the day and into the night, with tons of rock being shifted by Buck and three other helpers. Finally, darkness forced them off the fell, but Frank was back at the spot by first light, with help arriving a little later. Work began immediately on that Tuesday morning and by early afternoon around fifteen tons of rock and earth had been shifted from that fellside. By one o'clock Chew could at last be reached and the terrier was lifted out to great cheers of relief, though Tex still remained trapped. Frank called to his faithful terrier, which was now eight years of age and had accounted for literally hundreds of foxes, and Tex began climbing up the almost vertical sides of the rocks. However, just before Frank could get hold of him, Tex fell back in. Buck, never one to be defeated, got himself right into the crevice and, by almost hanging upside down, was able to at last get a hold of his terrier and bring it up to safety. The terriers had been to ground for over thirty hours and tons of rock had been shifted. They had managed to dig for a distance of twelve feet under the crag. This was just one of many rescues Frank Buck took part in and such rescues demonstrate the lengths these hunters would go to in order to protect the livestock of their beloved Dales country.

Prince Charles visited the West of Yore and hunted with them when Frank Buck was terrierman for this pack. Max Buck's terriers now work with this pack, though he also, like his father, removes foxes for keepers and farmers. Max has the last terrier that was in Frank's kennels when he died; a small Border/Fell type, which was unentered when Max took her in. He stated that she was rather slow to catch on, but she is now a very good finder and bolter of foxes. This terrier, Pip, was bred near Sedbergh, but Max in unsure of exactly who it was that bred her.

Max has worked terriers from being a lad, as one would expect really, and his job as a postman has meant that he could be finished for lunchtime when he would head straight to where hounds were hunting. On some occasions a fox had been 'run in' and he had missed his opportunity, but this happened very rarely, for Max was usually in time to work his terriers. He is

Max Buck with Pip, the last terrier in Frank's kennel when he died.

retired now, however, and so has plenty of time for following hounds and working his terriers with the pack where his father served for so long.

Max, like his father before him, never enters a terrier too early. He much prefers waiting until a dog is eighteen months of age before starting it at fox and he usually enters straight to this quarry, though a young entry may see the odd rat, or even a mink, before seeing its more traditional prey. He tries to give a youngster an easy first dig and this does wonders for their confidence.

I am extremely grateful to Max Buck for the time he spent showing me old photographs and talking about his father's strain of terrier, for Max is possibly *the* most important interviewee for this book. Being the eldest son of Frank Buck he has enjoyed a lifetime's interest in terriers and has actually helped in some measure in the development of the Buck/Breay breeding programme. He knew Cyril Breay very well and still has in his possession a tie pin which Mr Breay gave him for his twenty-first birthday, and, more importantly, he actually dug to Breay's terriers on several occasions. Max said that his father, a rather rough character who was a bit of a handful in his youth, was always more refined in speech and behaviour whenever he was in the company of Mr Breay or Donald Sinclair, both of whom were real gentlemen. Not that Buck was belligerent at other times, for he was a friendly, outgoing sort of chap, but Max agreed when I stated that 'you wouldn't have knocked his beer over'.

I photographed the terriers now belonging to Max and they are very much of a type that Frank was breeding years ago and they are well-socialised dogs with pleasant personalities. They are quite typey too as all go back to Daz, the bitch sired by Hardasty's Turk. I thoroughly enjoyed my trip to Leyburn to have a priviledged peep into the life of Frank Buck and Cyril Breay, two of the most famous breeders and workers of terriers. In fact, Frank must rate as one of the best terriermen ever produced in this country and his experience was equalled by very few. Buck and Breay have left us a legacy that is now treasured among working terrier folk, for they still retain those characteristics so beloved by their creators. Work came first, of course, but many of these terriers are suited to showing and, indeed, many terrier lads enjoy nothing more than visiting different venues throughout the summer off-season and competing in the show ring.

7

PATTERDALES
AND SHOWS

Showing can be a rather competitive business. We all hope that our terrier will be considered the best on the day and so it can be disappointing when sometimes you do not even get a rosette. Frank Buck and Cyril Breay won many top shows and when I was at Max Buck's house the pride Mr Breay felt for his top-winning terriers was much in evidence. Breay had sent Frank a postcard with a picture of Skiffle winning a championship and he had written on the back how the bitch had also won everything at Patterdale. Frank also won a lot of shows with his terriers, but he couldn't always decipher a good show terrier.

Max told me a tale of how Frank had given Brian Nuttall one of his terriers because he just couldn't take to it. At a show soon afterwards the terrier now belonging to Nuttall beat Frank's dog in their class and Max says that his father was not amused, though I could see by the way Max giggled mischievously that this had rather amused *him*.

Buck and Breay bred many very classy terriers and it is obvious that along the way they had included some rather typey Lakeland terrier blood in their breeding programme, for some of their stock would certainly win well today. Max confirmed that this was so, but he could not remember who it was that supplied the more classy Lakeland blood. Do not forget, Buck and Breay bred terriers in massive quantities and all sorts went into the mix, so it seems reasonable to suggest that they tidied up many of their terriers with the inclusion of more typey Lakeland terrier blood. For instance, Hardasty's Turk certainly went into the mix through the bitch Daz, which belonged to Max Buck, and much of the later show winning blood was undoubtedly descended from the union 'twixt Tina and Turk.

Barry Wild smartened his black stuff by using Middleton blood

An unregistered Lakeland of a type which gave rise to the pedigree Lakeland terrier.

in the main and he has won most of the top shows with his terriers. He bred Cassy, a black bitch which is now with Shane Sutton who won the Great Yorkshire show with this outstanding bitch a few years ago. I hunted with Cassy and she was a promising youngster, but, alas, is now living the life of a show dog, rather than a working animal. Cassy is a nuisance in kennel and will not settle; a result of not being allowed to exercise her natural hunting instinct!

Barry believes that his terriers are neither Patterdales, nor black Fell terriers, preferring to call them black Lakelands instead. They are very much a Lakeland in shape, but, being black, will inevitably be labelled as Patterdales, or black Fell terriers. He tells a tale of a show he attended which was being judged by Frank Buck. Barry put his elegant black terrier in the Lakeland class and Buck, never one to keep his opinion to himself, told Barry to take it out of the ring and put it in the crossbred class. Shortly afterwards Barry attended a show in South Yorkshire that was being judged by Jack Smith. His black terrier was now entered in the crossbred class and Smith told Barry to take it out of the ring and put it in the Lakeland class! Such is the confusion that goes on at working terrier shows.

The truth of the matter is that black is not a recognised colour for Lakeland terriers and the original Lakeland, the more typey coloured terrier which gave rise to the pedigree Lakeland, was never black, but either black and tan, or red, with a few variations such as wheaten, blue and tan, or red grizzle. I am sure the odd black terrier did appear, but these would have been either put down, or sold on as working terriers. Middleton says that most of the black stuff around in the early days was either Bedlington bred, or Bull terrier bred. So black terriers remain either Patterdales, or simply black Fell terriers.

My opinion is that, yes, black terriers originally bred by Buck and Breay are simply a type of Fell terrier, but the name Patterdale is so widely used today that it is pointless to try to alter this. Besides, the terriers produced by this pair are so distinctive that they deserve their own separate name, just as the Plummer terrier has been named seperately from the Jack Russell terrier. True, 'Patterdale terrier' is a name which is not really an accurate title, for the Patterdale district has only slight connections with this type of earth dog. Though terriers from this area certainly entered into the Buck/Breay breeding programme, for this part of the Lakes always produced the very best workers; when the Wilkinsons and the Barkers were actively breeding top class lookers and workers.

It is also a mistake to think that the name 'Patterdale terrier' can only be used in connection with smooth haired, untypey terriers unsuited to showing. I saw many terriers in old photos when I visited Max and the vast majority were incredibly typey harsh coated dogs which would easily compete even against the very best blacks today, and the best blacks today are being bred by Barry Wild, Mark Hallet and Danny Sykes. So if 'Patterdale terrier' is a name now inextricably linked to the dogs of Frank Buck and Cyril Breay, which is undoubtedly the case, then that name should also apply to the more typey terrier too.

There is much confusion in knowing which class to enter today. A black terrier may not always be catered for and the crossbred class can often be a mixture of all kinds of differing tykes. Some will put on classes for black Fell terriers, while their litter brothers and sisters that are red will go in the crossbred class. This is a

A Patterdale type being judged in the crossbred class.

ridiculous state of affairs, but is set to continue until standards are properly sorted out.

Some show venues also put on classes for Patterdale terriers and I have seen terriers from the same breeding split up into different classes in this situation too. For one thing, rough coated red terriers from the same litter as a smooth coated red, will not be considered as a Patterdale, but will be put into the crossbred class. However, a smooth black and a harsh coated black will be considered as Patterdale terriers. I do not have any solutions to the mess one sees in different classes at working terrier shows, but one thing is for sure, the increasing number of black terriers must be catered for by including either black Fell, or Patterdale terrier classes at the venue, along with the usual crossbred class of course.

A similar problem exists with Jack Russells. I have seen a judge throw a black and white terrier out of the crossbred class, telling the owner to put it in the Russell class, despite the handler telling him that it was a Patterdale cross Russell. If a Jack Russell judge knew of this, he would throw it out of the ring and tell the owner to put it into the crossbred class. This state of much confusion is set to continue, but shows must cater for all.

When I ran quite a number of shows I always attempted to provide classes for the large variety of terriers that were brought to these venues. Regarding Fell terriers, I put on classes for Lakelands, Fell terriers (a class encompassing crossbreds as well as red Patterdales etc) and Black Fell terriers (rough and smooth coated). This usually kept everyone happy, but still, sometimes it is hard to know which class is suited to a particular terrier. May I suggest that a possible solution to this problem is to put on classes for black Patterdales, splitting them between rough and smooth coated, and a class for all other colours (red, chocolate, bronze), rough and smooth coated. Any terrier bred out of Buck/Breay stock could be entered in such classes and just maybe a little of the confusion would then be cleared up!

Barry Wild believes that shows have in no way ruined the working qualities of terriers. Lack of work is what has ruined them, he says. This is true if the exhibitor has only used working stock to breed his exhibits, but if pedigree blood is used to smarten up a strain of terrier, then non-workers will undoubtedly result, for most of the pedigree stock today has very little hunting instinct. Barry likes a dog to be pleasing to the eye and believes that the unregistered type of Lakeland terrier (the type bred by such notables as Arthur Irving, Sid Wilkinson and Gary Middleton) is the yardstick of show dogs.

Many have succeeded in producing both top working and top winning stuff. Buck and Breay certainly succeeded in this, as has Gary Middleton, Graham Ward, Barry Wild, Mark Hallet, Wendy Pinkney, Ken Gould and, more recently, Danny Sykes. Danny now earns a living as a pest control officer and he uses his terriers in this capacity, actually getting paid for digging foxes with his terriers, just as Frank Buck was paid for controlling fox numbers throughout the Dales those many years ago. He does much digging with Dave Mitchell whose terriers go back to the original stock bred by Frank Buck and Cyril Breay, with a hint of Brightmore black stuff which were a mixture of Middleton and Buck/Breay breeding.

A black dog, Dodger, and a Dave Mitchell bred bitch, Skiffle, are the foundation stock for all of Danny's present terriers which are both workers and lookers. His smooth red dog, Brick, is a typey terrier of a sort that Buck would have been proud to own and he is also a superb worker. Tonic is another very typey animal, but all of Danny's stuff is used for work and they work foxes regularly throughout the winter. Like myself, Danny works his terriers to fox above and below ground. Danny told me a curious tale of a recent visit to a house after he had been called in, in order to carry out pest control.

He had taken his pistol along after a woman had telephoned to say she had a rat in her kitchen. Once in the house, she told him it had gone behind the fridge-freezer. Dodger, now getting on a bit, was in the car and he said that he would shoot it if she preferred, but that he had his dog in the car, which would sort out the problem in no time. She agreed to let the dog have a go and Danny then moved the fridge-freezer. Dodger shot behind and quickly killed the skulking rat. Even the most ardent opposer of hunting will be glad to see a rat off by any means possible!

The standard of judging at many shows is now very poor indeed. I was showing at a local event last year and I won my class with Fell, with Danny Sykes' red terrier, Brick, being placed second to my dog. And then, in the best-entered class, Brick won and Fell was placed second – by the very same judge. Inconsistency in judging is just one of the problems one sees today. At that same show, Fell was given reserve champion to a black dog which would have had difficulty getting into a bear's cave, let alone a fox earth. The dog must have been eighteen inches in height and was unspannable, having a huge chest and broad, Bull terrier-like shoulders. When I asked the judge how on earth such a dog could be placed before Fell, who is thirteen inches, easily spannable, has a strong head and weather-proof jacket, and is also a superb worker, I was told that if he was going to breed from a dog, it would have been the one he had put up as champion, for it was strong and chunky. If one breeds from a terrier that just cannot get to ground, a large percentage of its offspring will also be incapable of getting to a fox. A terrier stud should be of the correct size and should have those qualities needed to work below ground. Any terrier that cannot get to a fox in an average-sized earth should never be used as a stud.

Barry Wild, a top winning exhibitor of working terriers who has been showing successfully for many years, likes a terrier to be short-coupled and square, but without the over-exaggerated box shape of a pedigree Lakeland, many of which are so square that their chest is almost sticking out of their backsides! He likes a terrier to be more natural than that, for agility is vital in a terrier which works below ground, especially in rockpiles and borrans where a dog must twist and turn all over the place if it is going to negotiate the passages and follow its fox until it bolts, or settles in one place. Barry has worked many rockpiles with his classy terrier strain and they have acquitted themselves well in such earths. If shows are producing terriers that are just not agile enough to be capable of such feats, then, in my view, shows are ruining working terriers; as is the case with some of the pedigree breeds. Some of these are so square and stiff that they would have absolutely no chance of working a difficult spot.

A Patterdale terrier should please the eye. In other words, it should neither be too long in the back, nor too short and squat in the body, but just right. It should move freely, not as stiff as a board. The head should be strong, the jaw powerful and with ears that are not too large, nor too small, but in balance with the general head-size. The legs should be straight and well-muscled, the shoulders powerful, but not so large that they prevent a terrier from getting into an average sized fox hole, and the chest should be spannable; though a judge must be discerning when spanning terriers. If one has small hands, then a bit of give and take can be applied, for a terrier that cannot be fully spanned by small hands will undoubtedly still get to its fox. A judge who is experienced in the field, rather than in the ring, is the one who knows instinctively what is, and what is not, capable of working below ground.

The jacket should be dense and tight to the skin, whether smooth or rough, and should be coarse to the touch, rather than soft and silky. A jacket of this type is lethal to a terrier working below ground during mid-winter, especially in the uplands where sudden storms and freezing temperatures can cause havoc to a dog with not enough protection from its coat.

Barry Wild likes a terrier to be fiery in the ring, but I much prefer a quieter sort, the type that gets along with other terriers well and can be worked in small packs. This is especially important when ratting, or bushing rabbits. My terriers are reluctant to fight, but they are eager workers above and below. There should be plenty of fire in a terrier roused by fox scent, but in the ring, the home, or out at exercise, I much prefer a placid terrier. In the world of working terriers it is a case of 'each to his own'.

A working terrier should have a natural scissor-bite, though an undershot mouth – the most common fault in working terriers today – will in no way effect a terrier's ability below ground, for the bite is still as strong and effective. An undershot mouth is a fault, nevertheless, but it should not be considered as a serious fault. I know of undershot dogs being given even the championship by some judges. And I would do the same if the faults of the other dogs were worse. For instance, I would put an undershot exhibit ahead of one with a poor coat every time. Why? Because a terrier with a poor coat will suffer badly and may even die if trapped to ground in bad weather for any length of time, while an undershot terrier is still capable of killing a fox that refuses to bolt. One must weigh-up the bad and good points and come to a decision.

One thing I do not agree with, and I have seen it often, is picking out a terrier simply because it is battle-scarred. I was once in the championship with a red dog, Crag. This terrier was thirteen inches at the shoulder, he had a good, strong head and one of the tightest, harshest jackets I have ever seen on a terrier. He was also a very good worker, being a good finder and a stayer during digs, though he wasn't a hard dog. He would not kill a fox, but still, he would put the pressure on, working close to his quarry, while avoiding serious injury. The judge was a young lad who had been working terriers for four years! At that time I had sixteen years experience behind me. The dog that was given the championship was an almost pure Bull terrier (it was labelled as a Patterdale) with many fresh scars (unhealed) all over its face.

Scars can be picked up in kennel fights and many of them are. Wendy Pinkney's bitch, Briar, although a superb worker who served at fox for several seasons, had part of her lip missing, not through work, but because a young terrier seized her through the bars of a terrier-box and bit it off. So never pick a winner according to the number of scars it carries. True, a worker will get bitten at times and sometimes quite badly when a fox has a stronghold from where it will not budge, but the wounds will heal and most scars will usually be covered over when the hair grows back (a slape coated terrier will show scars far more than does a rough coated dog). For instance, my bitch, Mist, has been bitten a few times on the lips, but no scars remain. Scars very often show for quite some time afterwards when bites are received on the muzzle, but those on lips and nose will soon be gone, so looking for scars is a poor measure when it comes to judging at

Frank Buck's Great Yorkshire Show winner – a terrier bred
down from Daz (Tina x Hardasty's Turk).

shows. And, if a judge is so obviously making poor decisions, do
not be afraid to approach him (or her) and ask the reason why
such and such a decision was made, if you are not happy. If you
do approach a judge, always make sure that you are not pulling
him up over trivialities, or because you are disappointed at not
winning. Judges should be questioned when blatantly wrong
decisions are made.

Patterdale terriers are treasured far more for their working
ability than for how successful they are in the show ring. And so
further addition of other terrier blood is undesirable, for the

working qualities may be adversely affected. Buck/Breay blood-lines must not be weakened any further by putting Bull terrier, the most common outcross, or pedigree Lakeland blood (used to improve type) into Patterdale terriers. By breeding to related Patterdale stock, breeders today can keep the bloodlines of the original strains running strong. This can be achieved by keeping working qualities first and foremost. Remember, this type of terrier did well at shows with Buck and Breay and by continuing to breed from this stock one is sure to keep producing at least some stuff that is typey enough to be competitive at shows. However, if you do decide to improve type, then try to find a smart stud dog which is at least related to the Buck/Breay strain of terrier and which is a proven worker.

8

PATTERDALES AND THE FAMILY

Although primarily a working dog, the Patterdale terrier also makes a great pet. Both Frank Buck and Cyril Breay were family men and they would not have tolerated terriers that could not be trusted within the family arrangement. True, most of their dogs were kennelled, but their children helped out with caring for them and, with the Bucks in particular, helped out when hunting (Max Buck cannot remember ever seeing Breay's children out hunting with him). Frank's sons whipped-in at the Wensleydale harriers whenever their father was acting foot Huntsman.

I believe that Patterdales have such lovely temperaments because of the large amount of Border terrier blood that features so heavily in their pedigree. Border terriers at both the Bedale hunt and the Zetland, most being three-quarter bred Borders, entered the Buck/Breay breeding programme, as did the almost pure Border, Akerigg's Lasty, which was mated by Bingo on several occasions and produced a large amount of the later slape coated Patterdales which were both typey and very game. Border terriers are notoriously quiet and reserved in nature and they are also incredibly suited as children's pets.

The early Border terrier was a superb worker and Buck's Tex, possibly the best worker Frank ever owned, carried quite a few lines back to Border terriers. It is such outcross blood that is to thank for the calm and docile nature of modern Patterdales, which make them ideal family pets. Of course, a Patterdale can quite easily fill a double role; that of pet and working dog at the same time, though there is an increasing number of people who are keeping Patterdales just as pets, in both Britain and America.

When one has owned a Patterdale terrier it is easy to understand why this is so. They have very pleasant, cheerful personalities and they are quiet, docile creatures which love to curl up in front of the fire, or, preferably, on their owner's lap. However, they are also full of life and inquisitiveness. In fact, this inquisitiveness can also lead them into mischief.

A couple of years ago a news report came on television telling of a terrier, a family pet, not a working dog, that had disappeared into a hole and failed to return. A digging machine was brought in and the hillside dug up until, at last, and to the great relief of the owner, a young lad, the terrier was recovered safe and sound. I recognised the dog immediately as being a Patterdale terrier of Brian Nuttall's breeding, for they are so distinctive as to be easily recognised.

Patterdale terriers, because they have such a long and unbroken pedigree as working dogs, are natural hunters and, when they mature, will take to hunting should the opportunity arise, whether the owner likes it or not. This can present a danger to an owner who is not familiar with the wildlife of their country. For instance, in Britain it is illegal to hunt badgers and the simple act of allowing a terrier to enter a badger sett is enough to bring the full might of the law down on one's head like a ton of bricks. The innocent pet owner out walking and enjoying the beauty and

Ghyll checking out the world beyond the window. Pups must become familiar with cats, other dogs, etc, as soon as vaccinations are completed.

peace of the countryside, could so easily find themselves in trouble if their terrier disappeared into a sett.

For this reason it is best to know the ground where one walks the terrier like the back of your hand. If you do not, then the best option is to keep the dog on a lead. When I was the area representative for the Mid-Lancs area of the Fell and Moorland Working Terrier Club I was called out by an elderly couple, whose Border terrier had gone missing while out walking in woodland.

I took my old bitch, Rock, with me and began searching through the woods and the undergrowth. The elderly couple were not members of the club, but were simply pet owners who were out exercising their beloved dog and enjoying a breath of fresh country air. The dog, they said, had caught the scent of something and had run off through the trees. I searched everywhere, trying every earth I came across with my terrier, but no trace could be found of the Border and it was never seen again. Three possible explanations were now put to the couple :

(1) The terrier had run off, probably chasing a fox, for there were plenty of earths in that wood and many signs of fox activity, and had been picked up by someone thinking the dog was lost.

(2) The dog had been seen by someone and was then stolen.

(3) The terrier had got itself into a rabbit hole, fox earth, or badger sett and had become trapped below ground, or had suffocated after digging onto its quarry.

As one can imagine, the couple were terribly upset and did all they could to track down their pet, but were unsuccessful. One can only assume that the third option was the most likely! This is not always the case, however, for some mistakenly think that a terrier is lost to ground when, in actual fact, it has emerged, strayed, and has been picked up by someone who has either kept it themselves, or has passed it onto a dogs' home. If one loses a terrier to ground, it is always worth checking local police stations and dogs' homes, as well as putting a photo in local shops etc, just in case.

Any kind of hunting dog, when kept as a pet, can take to hunting whether the owner approves, or otherwise. An elderly gentleman who lived on the estate where I was born and raised, owned a Border cross Jack Russell and the dog did nothing but hunt. As soon as it was off the lead it was away with its nose to the ground, chasing rabbits all over the place and almost wiping out the local hedgehog population by turning them over and killing them, much in the same way as a badger will kill them. Patterdales are the same. They have an incredibly strong hunting instinct and need to be watched, even kept on the lead, while out at exercise in areas where there is a danger of your dog getting into a hole, especially such places as badger setts.

Patterdale terriers, because of their quiet, docile nature, can be quite sensitive and need careful handling. Terriers have strong personalities generally, so one must be firm when raising and training a puppy, but one must also be aware of the sensitive nature of this type of terrier and not be overbearing, making them nervous and shy and knocking their self-confidence for six. The best way of handling them is to give plenty of praise when they do the right thing, and show your disapproval firmly, but without uncontrolled anger, when they do wrong. A smack on their backsides will do no harm when it comes to more serious wrongdoing, but one must avoid being too heavy handed. I generally use a light swish for disciplining bad behaviour as this will sting, but will do no harm at all. By praising good behaviour, the animal will associate pleasantness with that good behaviour, and by using a swish, or firm words of disapproval, the dog will associate unpleasantness with such behaviour and will thus avoid doing those things that bring its master's disapproval.

An untrained and undisciplined terrier will cause its owner much grief. The loving thing to do is to shape the terrier into a well behaved, trustworthy adult. For instance, if cats are a common pet in your area and are likely to be encountered while your dog is off the lead, then break it to cats. Do this early on, while it is still a puppy, and reinforce the training as the puppy grows and matures (for more advice on training, see *The Traditional Working Terrier*). If you will be using ferrets in conjunction with your terrier, then break it to ferrets too. If you will not be working your terrier, but there are people in your area who walk their pet ferret on a lead, then still break to ferrets, for the last thing you want is for your terrier to kill someone's beloved pet. Patterdales are hunting dogs through and through, but still, it is easy enough to teach them what is, and what is not, acceptable to hunt.

Daisy and Yasmine with Fell. Spending time with children is a vital part of the socialising process.

Socialise, socialise, socialise; that is the key to a well behaved, trustworthy pet, or, indeed, working dog. This responsibility to begin socialising a puppy rests with the breeder first of all. From very early on, as soon as the bitch will allow it in fact, the breeder should be handling the puppies on a regular basis, though, obviously, very gently. As they grow, the breeder should play with the whole litter regularly too. If there are children in the family, these too should be handling the pups from an early age, though always under strict supervision from an adult. However, if regular handling is upsetting the bitch, then make the sessions a little less frequent.

As the puppies grow they will become evermore playful and children will delight in handling and playing with them. This means that, by the time the puppies are old enough to be sold at eight weeks of age, they will be very familiar with children and with being handled generally. Those first few weeks are vital to raising a well-socialised terrier puppy. Children love nothing better than carrying puppies around and dressing them up like dolls and this should be encouraged, as long as the child is

167

Home comforts.

old enough to know how to handle a pup gently and carefully enough so as not to be dropping it. When I bred a litter out of Fell and Mist last year, I encouraged Yasmine and Daisy, our grand-daughters, to play with the pups as they grew. Yasmine really took to Beck and was constantly carrying her around and treating her like a doll. At first, Beck resisted and struggled to get away from her, but it wasn't long before she began going totally limp and allowed Yasmine to just get on with it. I have seen Beck lying under a quilt designed for a doll and with her head on a miniature pillow, being treated like a doll that has just been put to bed. Such contact between children and puppies, as long as the child is taught how to gently handle a pup, will ensure an adult dog which can be fully trusted around children.

My sister, Elizabeth, grew up from being a baby surrounded by dogs and another terrier I bred, Bella, was treated like a doll also, being constantly carried around and dressed up in dolls' clothing. Bella would growl almost continuously, but only in protest, for she was sound with children and never even attempted to bite.

Socialising, as we have seen, begins in the home and a puppy should soon become familiar with children and adults alike, having become used to visitors descending on them and making a fuss of them. But still, after the innoculations have been completed, a puppy needs to become more familiar with people and their world. This is easily done. Just take the puppy to areas where there are plenty of folk around; public parks, even into town where people are shopping. Do this quite regularly during those first few months and your pup will soon take the crowds in its stride.

One of the most important lessons a puppy can learn is to accept the presence of other dogs without turning aggressive. Again, take your terrier to places where other dogs will be encountered, places such as parks and even dog shows. If you will be exhibiting your dog, then it is best to get it familiar with the show environment early on, but the main objective is for them to meet other dogs. Your local vet may know of a puppy play-group you can attend. This may sound a bit daft, but they are good ideas for those who care about raising well-behaved, properly socialised pets and working animals, though the working terrier enthusiast can do no better than attend country

Patterdales love to be on their owner's lap.

shows on a regular basis where the puppy will meet all types of dogs and will soon take these meetings in their stride.

Raising a pleasant dog is vital. One that is aggressive to other dogs, and shy with people, will be a great nuisance to its owner and other folk alike. For instance, a terrier which chases cars is a danger to itself and to the public. By walking the youngster alongside busy roads regularly as it grows, you will avoid this occurrence, for your puppy will soon learn to ignore traffic, deeming it irrelevant to their world. So the energy one puts into that first year of a terrier's life is well worth the effort, for you will have a dog, whether it be a pet, working dog, or both, that will bring you great pleasure over the years to come.

Clare Sawers, the marketing manager at Quiller Publishing, has Patterdales and she finds them to be wonderful family pets; biddable, great with kids and easily managed. Her bitch, Dilly, was bred by Nick Stevens and Nick told her that, if he gave her Dilly, she mustn't breed from her unless first she had been entered to fox. Clare agreed and Dilly, once she was old enough, was then put into hunt service under the expert guidance of Dave Finlay and served for a full season. Clare's present Patterdales are a mixture of Nick Stevens and Dave Finlay bloodlines. Despite the strong working background of these terriers (both Nick and Dave are professional terriermen), they are still well suited to life as pets.

9
PATTERDALES IN AMERICA

Brian Nuttall sent the first Patterdale terriers to America in 1978; a bitch in pup and a six-month old dog. These were purchased by Al Wolfe, who wrote under the penname of 'Boston Blackie'. Since then, Brian has sent several Patterdales to America where they are now growing in popularity, both as working dogs and as pets. Pit Bull terriers and Airedale terriers have been popular working dogs in America for many years, but now, in several cases, they are losing ground to Patterdales. There is good reason for this.

Many of the creatures which are hunted in America can cause great damage to a foolhardy dog which lacks sense and attacks quarry, taking severe punishment rather than standing back and working their quarry more sensibly. This is why Patterdales are becoming evermore popular for hunting even very large quarry. Wild pigs are hunted in America and these can be savage prey to a dog which lacks sense. Many of the working Airedales and Pit Bull terriers, though extremely courageous, have no reverse gears and are often mauled badly, sometimes fatally.

The American hunting enthusiasts then began finding that Patterdales were just as game (possibly even more game), facing quarry far larger than themselves, but without taking serious maulings. Many strains of British Patterdales can work foxes, and even finish them below ground, without taking too much punishment, and this sense has stood them in good stead out in the wilds of America.

The raccoon is also on the quarry list in America and these can be quite fierce creatures for a terrier to deal with. Middleton has sent dogs from his strain to America for the hunting of quarry such as raccoons, American badgers and their more traditional quarry, foxes. Many of Nuttall's stock have also gone out there for the same purpose. Raccoons will raid farmyards as eagerly as will a fox and they can cause devastation if they get into a chicken run. Some farmers and smallholders are now using Patterdales for protecting their livestock from predators and foxes, raccoons and even skunk have been accounted for by simply having a

Brian Nuttall with Buster.

terrier running loose around the place. The raccoon is about the size of a badger and they can bite hard and do much damage to an unwary terrier.

Terriers have been used in this same manner on British farms for millenniums, rather than centuries, and have done a superb job of keeping predators at bay. At one time almost every farm would have a terrier or two (some farms had small packs of terriers about the place when I was a lad), running loose around the premises, both in order to deter predators, and thieves, but nowadays far fewer farms have terriers in residence. The terrier packs on the farms I worked at as a young lad did a cracking job of keeping rat numbers down to a minimum.

The American badger, about the same size as its European cousin, is also hunted with Patterdales and a terrier must have sense if it is to work such a creature without getting too badly knocked about, or even killed. Badgers have a great deal of fight in them and a dog that tackles such creatures head-on is going to come unstuck. So sense is rated highly by American hunters, just as highly, in fact, as the old time fell-hunters who had the job of keeping the local fox population in check, despite impossible conditions, terrain and earths.

Because there is plenty of large quarry in America, the hunting enthusiasts prefer their hunting dogs to be both game and strong. This is another reason why Patterdales have become more popular in recent years. They like the Bull terrier looks about a Patterdale, for they know that the influence of such blood enables an earth dog to stand its ground against prey that is far larger and heavier. For instance, although a Patterdale may weigh only thirteen or fourteen pounds, they are still capable of holding an American badger at a stop end, or even drawing it out of a bad spot, despite the fact that such creatures will weigh between thirty and forty pounds. In certain spots in the Lake District, Gary Middleton would dig down to his terrier, only to find that the badger was under a large, unmoveable rock. Middleton's terriers, although no heavier than seventeen pounds, were then required to draw Brock from under that rock. It is an incredible feat for such small dogs.

The strength of these small earth dogs, the handy size which means they can get even into very tight places, the boundless amount of courage and, more especially, the sense while up to quarry that far outweighs them, are the qualities that have made these terriers more and more popular in America. But they are not popular just as working dogs, for quite a number, a growing number in fact, are keeping these charming little terriers as pets.

Patterdale terriers are reluctant to fight and make great pets, for they are quiet around the house and love children. They are very patient, tolerant dogs and will put up with rough treatment from a young child, though children must be taught to handle dogs gently.

Although Patterdale terriers have temperaments that make them ideal as pets, it is also true to say that, if one wishes to have a well behaved, trustworthy pet, then it is essential to make certain that they do not become bored. Bored terriers can become problems and so it is vital to keep them occupied and thus happy. Plenty of exercise and play will keep a terrier contented. For instance, throwing a ball in a park will help a terrier burn off excess energy and keep its mind occupied too, for chasing that ball will be just as exciting for a terrier as chasing a rabbit. Allowing children to play with a Patterdale terrier will keep both the dog and them happy, for all concerned will sleep at night, having burned off plenty of energy.

Patterdales can be kept anywhere, in large and small houses, trailer homes, even apartments, as long as they are kept happy, either with work, or plenty of exercise and play, for they are not yappy dogs. Also, they have jackets that do not shed too much hair, are cleaned easily, and maintained with hardly any effort; just a good brushing once or twice a week to remove dead hair. They are a delight to have around the home as they have friendly, cheerful personalities and are quiet, so quiet, in fact, that you hardly know they are there.

Max Buck is certain that his father sent some of his terriers to America, but he cannot remember exactly when this was so. Frank Buck did not view them as Patterdale terriers and so he would not have sent them out there as such. If he did send any of his stock to America, and this seems very likely, then they would have been sent simply as Fell terriers. If this occurred before 1978, then this type of terrier had already reached America before Nuttall's terriers. Finding out the truth of this matter, however, is now an impossibility but that doesn't really matter, for the Patterdale terrier is now well established in America.

Besides Al Wolfe, there have been quite a number of importers of Patterdale terriers and the vast majority have turned to Brian Nuttall to supply them with such terriers, though Ken Gould has also sent a few out to America where they have acquitted them-

Patterdales are quiet and reserved and get along with other dogs.

selves well, as workers in the main. Mary-Ann Hauk (a keeper of accurate pedigrees concerning Patterdales), Benny Benson of California, Sid Birt, David Myers and Dave Lindsey are just a few who have pioneered the breeding and working of Patterdale terriers in America.

A large number are now being bred in that country, but a large number have also been imported by such breeders. A few of the terriers to be exported to America by Nuttall were Rocky, Tiger, Tarmac and Nickel, amongst many others, and pregnant bitches and puppies have also been sent out there.

There are now a good number of websites concerning Patterdales in America, but, because sites can be constantly changing, new ones being set up and old ones becoming defunct, I will not list these here. The best method is to do a search by clicking onto an internet company such as Google, and simply type in *Patterdale terriers usa*, and the whole list of sites will appear. On such sites, one can get info about clubs, societies and shows, as well as current breeders. Also, links to websites in other countries can be found amongst the information contained on these sites.

Patterdales have also reached several parts of Europe and, as is the case in America, are growing in popularity. They are used for, among other things, wild boar hunting and this says something of the sense these terriers possess, for a headstrong dog with no sense, a 'fool-game' sort of disposition, would come unstuck when hunting such large, fierce quarry. Like the Americans, the Europeans are finding the Patterdale terrier to be an ideal working dog and, in many cases, a more than suitable pet. Let us hope that both the working side of the Patterdale's life, and the pet side too, continues to grow and becomes ever-more popular. They may be one of the rarest breeds in America at the moment, but that situation could be about to change!

10

THE PUPPY
AND ITS TRAINING

Choice of puppy

Choosing a puppy is a serious business and it is essential to get this right first time. Do not rush this. When arriving at the breeder's house, take your time. Do not go for the first pup you see, hand your money over and rush home to begin settling it in. Instead, sit down and observe. A breeder will not mind you taking time to choose, if you choose at all that is, and so do not feel pressured to buy. If you are being pressured by a breeder, then take your leave, for he has little interest in the welfare of his puppies and just wishes to be rid of them. If you can get the address of a well-known breeder who has a good reputation, then book a puppy from such a source. If you are going to work the animal, then always buy from one who works their stock and will only breed from proven workers.

Make certain that the litter is clean and healthy, the bitch obviously well cared for. The eyes of a healthy pup will be bright, shiny and alert. The coat should be glossy and full, without the skin showing through, or any bald patches. The litter should be playful and full of energy. If a puppy is listless, it will either be generally unhealthy, or it may have a heart defect, so stay clear of any pup not readily joining in play. I do not mean a shy puppy, however, for many Patterdales, from being young pups, can be reserved and a little timid. This is nothing to worry about and has no bearing on suitability as a pet, or as a working dog. In fact, some of the best workers I have owned have been shy and retiring, so do not let this put you off. Pick the one that appeals the most to you; this is the best advice I can give.

Taking the puppy home is an important business also. Do not throw it in the boot, lock it up in a dark place all alone and leave it until you get home. That could cause severe mental turmoil

Pups out of Dilly and Gomez.

which could so easily ruin the temperament of a puppy. The best thing to do is to take someone along with you, preferably not a young child for obvious reasons, who can hold the dog in their lap on the way home and keep it warm, comfortable and comforted. If you can, get some of the bedding to take home with you, or at least give the bitch a good stroking so that her scent is all over your hands, as this will help settle a puppy. If you cannot find a travelling companion, then take a deep cardboard box with an old towel and newspaper in the bottom, and place this on the floor of the passenger side with the top open, so that the puppy can see you. By all means, comfort the pup with a few soft words, but keep your eyes on the road, for both of you will want to arrive home safely!

Feeding
The breeder will usually give you a diet sheet and a gentle feed on arriving home is essential, for this will help to settle a puppy. Make this a small meal, maybe of cereal and slightly warmed milk. Puppy food and puppy biscuits will make up the other meals, which should be given at least three times per day. Breakfast should be of cereal and lunch of meat and biscuits, repeated again at tea-time. Of course, if you work full-time, then

you must work your feeding schedule around this. The important thing is that the youngster gets plenty of food at least three times in one day. This is a matter of common sense. If you feel the pup is getting too much, then reduce the feed, or if it is getting too little, increase the quantity, or go to four meals a day instead. A puppy should be neither thin nor fat, but 'plump' with excess weight, but not too much so that its health and its ability to play is affected.

By the age of four months, the lunchtime feed can be cut out. At eight months of age, I drop the breakfast and give just one meal a day from then on. This will be plenty, even for a very active terrier which works upwards of three or four days a week, though, after a hard day's work, I will increase the quantity somewhat, for a working terrier will burn off energy and excess fat incredibly quickly, especially during a long stint to ground. Puppy food and biscuits can be replaced with normal adult food at the age of six months and I feed meat and a mixer-meal from then on. Tinned meat is fine, as is brawn, but I must confess to not liking complete dog foods, for these are like rabbit feed and seem to make them defecate far more, which suggests there is more waste. Of course, when terriers are kept in large numbers, economy will dictate that these complete foods are used, for when bought in huge sacks the cost is far less, but for one or two terriers tinned meat and biscuits is fine and easily affordable.

Innoculations

With regard to innoculations, the best advice I can give is to telephone your veterinary surgeon and ask their advice, for in recent years much more effective vaccinations have come on the market and so ideas change. Not so long ago, these injections could not be started until a puppy was twelve weeks of age, but now they begin at eight weeks. Do not take them too soon, for the upheavel of finding themselves away from the bitch and siblings, along with a familiar environment, is enough to cope with for the first couple of days, without them being taken to the vet also.

It is essential to innoculate against Parvo-virus, Distemper and Leptospirosis (Weil's disease which is prevalent in rats) and always follow veterinary advice regarding these, for a puppy must not go out onto the streets, or into the countryside, until it is fully protected against such diseases. Of course, in some countries, vaccinations against Rabies is also essential, Again, speak to your vet about this matter.

Piper, a good strong pup.

Kennelling

Advice for housing is, again, based on common sense. If housing indoors, then provide a warm and comfortable area for your puppy to sleep in, such as a plastic dog bed. You could use a bed made of soft material, but your puppy may chew these and ruin them, so go for the hard plastic type until adulthood, when the risk of chewing is virtually nil. The bedding provided should be old newspapers (shredded paper is just as good) as these are warm and provide no opportunities for fleas to breed, unlike an old towel or sheet. They have the added attraction of being easily thrown away and replaced. Providing toys and cow-hide bones is an ideal way of keeping a puppy occupied during times when it is alone and this will also greatly reduce the risk of chewing, though it is always best to keep a puppy in an area where the opportunity to chew valuable furniture is not available.

If kennelling outside, then make certain that the structure is dry, draught-free and secure from the attentions of thieves. A concrete floor is the best option, for this is easily cleaned, but whatever type of kennel you choose, cleaning out the droppings two or three times a day and disinfecting it once a day is essential, especially during the warm summer months. Disinfection can take place a couple of times a week during winter when the risk of infection is much reduced. This applies to the floor of course, for the walls of the structure will only need doing once a month during summer and just once or twice through the winter. The bedding should be cleaned out and the bed (an enclosed box, for keeping out frost and draughts, with plenty of extra bedding in winter, is best) given a good clean once a week throughout the year. The kennel should consist of an enclosed area and an outside run and they should be roomy enough for the number of terriers kept there. For instance, where two are kept together, I would provide a kennel of 6ft by 3ft (1.8m by 1m)and a run of the same proportions, though a run of 6ft by 6ft (1.8m by 1.8m) is preferable. If you wish, you can place sawdust on the floor in order to soak up the urine and bad odours, though this must be swept and cleaned out at least once a day.

Early training
Socialising means getting a puppy to take everyday life in its stride. Children can fuss with them within reason. When a puppy is trying to sleep, then teach a child to leave it alone. While at play, make certain that your child handles the puppy gently. Also, teach a child not to fuss around a dog whilst it is feeding, for terriers are jealous and can snap at a child fussing around them while they are eating. Introducing the puppy to other animals is child's play, but keep a pup on your lap and well shielded from older dogs which may be a little too rough at first, until you have firmly told them to be gentle.

Playing with a pup is part of the socialising process.

With cats, a puppy will have to learn to keep its distance until accepted, though you can quickly teach a pup not to fuss around a cat too much by telling it to 'leave' whenever it approaches. The same lesson can be taught with ferrets too. Sternly warn your puppy to 'leave' a ferret alone, cracking a leather lead on the ground in front of it whilst doing so, for a working Patterdale must not hurt its hunting ally. *Never* leave a puppy alone with a ferret, however, for a fitch will attack such a vulnerable creature and easily kill it. The same principle applies with breaking to live-stock. Taking the puppy amongst sheep, cattle, horses, hens etc, not to mention domestic cats, and sternly warning it to 'leave', from the very day you begin exercising after innoculations, will ensure that an adult dog will not attack such creatures whilst at exercise, or out hunting.

Keeping a terrier healthy is essential and is easily accomplished. Provide clean housing, enough daily food, plenty of play and exercise (a walk of at least half an hour a day is essential, but two walks of such duration are far better and essential if one lives in an apartment where there is no garden), providing the necessary innoculations and keeping the animal free of fleas and worms, are the basic requirements. There are now very effective worm and flea treatments available at your vets, but these can be

A Patterdale well broken to cats; a good idea when so many cats are found in hunted areas and built up areas alike.

expensive. For puppies, I strongly recommend the puppy wormer in liquid form and chocolate flavoured (see chapter 11) and for adults the multi-wormer tablets from either the pet shop, or the vets, which are given a couple of times a year (always follow the instructions provided with such remedies).

Obedience training

Obedience training is part and parcel of the socialising process and is essential if one is to rear a dog with good manners. Along with plenty of play, getting your puppy familiar with both adults and children, a terrier must also be taught boundaries that must not be crossed and that means being fair, but firm.

The first thing a puppy must begin learning is to come to its master on command. Realistically, although immediate obedience is the ideal, this is something that is most unlikely in any of the common working breeds of terrier, including Patterdales, for

Pups learn necessary skills while playing with other dogs.

they are most strong-willed and are independent souls, so they often need a little 'persuasion'.

The late Brian Plummer often stressed that bending down and putting one's head near to the ground is a most effective way of getting a puppy to come to its master. I have found this to be so, but that effectiveness soon wears off. When the owner puts his or her face to the ground, their instinct tells them that they are going to receive food, for a puppy will lick its dam's mouth in order to stimulate her instinct to regurgitate partly digested food which is much easier for a puppy to tackle.

When the puppy discovers that no food results from its master simulating the actions of the bitch, it will soon become unresponsive and that method no longer works. Of course, one could reward the youngster on approach with little treats (dog chocolates are the best titbits to offer, though small biscuits manufactured especially for puppies are also effective), and this will keep a young dog responsive, but one still has to put in all of that effort in bending down and getting on one's knees: a pointless exercise, for a puppy will come just as keenly when called and given a treat, without the exertions involved in bending down and getting back up again.

After choosing a name for your puppy, simply call it to you with an appealing tone in your voice, which will arouse curiosity. An excited, higher-pitched tone is the most interesting to a pup and it will soon be on its way towards you. As it comes, continue using its name and keep up the same tone. Once it has come to you, give it plenty of praise and then reward it with a little titbit.

Continue doing this and very soon your youngster will be coming keenly when called, although, as I say, they will not usually respond immediately.

Sit, lie and stay are very easy lessons to teach and praise and rewards, coupled with fun play sessions, are the best ways of teaching a young dog, some of which learn very quickly indeed. After calling the puppy to you and having rewarded its obedience, simply press gently on its back-end whilst commanding it to 'sit'. After having rewarded its compliance as it yields to the pressure from your hand, repeat the lesson a few times, but keep the sessions short. Several sessions can be carried out throughout the day, but each session must not be long enough for a terrier to become bored and frustrated. A few minutes of play after each training session will also prevent boredom from setting in. Terriers have a mind of their own and if they are allowed to view training sessions as unpleasant affairs, then succeeding in getting obedience from your puppy is going to be very difficult indeed.

Once in the sit position, gently pull out the front legs while pushing down on the shoulders and utter the command to 'lie-down'. Once accomplished, and while the pup is still in the lie position, praise and reward its compliance. Puppies do not enjoy the lie-down position as much as the sit position and so it is best to keep this aspect of training a little shorter. By repeating this lesson frequently, however, boredom and frustration will be avoided and the lessons reinforced so that a puppy will learn extremely quickly what is required of it.

Getting a puppy to stay is much more difficult and a terrier, naturally curious and extremely active, will not wish to be stuck in one position and place for more than a second or so! And so it is vital to be firm and much praise and reward must be given, along with play of course, during such training. Teaching a dog to stay can be done in both the lie-down and the sit positions. Once a puppy is in the required position, put your hand in front of its face and command it to 'stay'.

All commands should be given in a firm tone of voice, which tells the pupil that its tutor will not stand any messing, otherwise you will not be taken seriously and the puppy will soon put up for 'boss' of its household. One must be firm if a puppy is to learn its place. Do not forget, dogs are pack animals and must know their place if a pack is to function properly. You must be pack leader and that means very quickly establishing your authority over the animal. Do not take any messing from a puppy. Make certain that your dog carries out the commands you give and accept nothing less, for some puppies will try to promote themselves to 'pack leader' as quickly as possible and unfortunately, in many households, they succeed. Do not allow this in your household, for terriers allowed to rule themselves, so to speak, will only cause endless problems for their owners.

At first, a puppy will try to move, so be firm and put it back in its place, while at the same time uttering the command to 'stay'. Repeating this through short sessions in the early stages will quickly teach a youngster that it is not to move until allowed to do so. And, once the 'stay' command is beginning to be clearly understood, one can lengthen the time that a puppy is required to stay until you are satisfied with the results.

House training

House training is simple enough, but one must have a great deal of patience when training a novice. In the beginning, a puppy will simply squat and either urinate or defecate without even thinking twice about it. You must act quickly and show the pup the mess, telling it 'no' in a firm tone while giving it a light tap on its backside. Then take the puppy outdoors and place it in the area you wish it to use as a toilet, telling it 'outside' as you do so. An old rag with a dash of disinfectant applied to it will be ideal for cleaning the floor (after the excrement has been removed of course) and removing offending odours. Keep this up persistently, never allowing your young dog to get away with messing unpunished, and it will not be long before it gets the idea. Some learn in days, while others can take weeks, but eventually they will not dirty in the house any more, though there may be an occasional accident and one must be quick to give the growing dog a sharp reminder in such circumstances.

Teaching a youngster not to use your floor as a toilet during the long nights, however, is far more difficult and this lesson, in some cases, may take a few months to learn. The best way of going about it is to allow the puppy to sleep in a confined area which is dry, relatively warm (but not close to radiators or any other kind of heater) draught-free and well ventilated. Place old newspaper on the floor and your puppy will use this as a toilet during the night. On rising, show the puppy the offending mess, tell it 'no' while tapping (gently) its backside with the end of your fingers and take it outside as already described.

Ghyll with Rock. Puppies can learn much from an older dog.

The mess will, in time, become less and less until, finally, you are rising to a clean floor. The newspaper can then be taken up and not put down again, for it was only there to make cleaning much easier. If, as is the case with some growing pups, the messing is persistent even after months of training, then one must resort to strict methods, which will end this problem. I am convinced that some dogs simply get into the habit of messing and so this cycle must be broken if housetraining is to succeed. A terrier box is ideal for this purpose. This box must be roomy enough for a dog to change position, but it must not have enough room so that it can mess in one corner and sleep in another, well away from its excrement, or urine. A dog will not usually wish to lie in its mess and so, thus confined, will hold itself until the morning, for an older dog has no problem holding itself for upwards of eight or nine hours, provided it is allowed either exercise, or a good roam around the garden, before going to bed.

A box should not be roomy enough for a bowl of fresh water to be placed inside, and so one must obtain a water bottle, of the type designed for rabbits, which can be attached to the mesh of the door in order that the youngster can have a drink during the night if it so wishes, though I have found that very little drink is taken during an average night. A dog will know by scent that it can get water from this source, but just to get things started, give the bottle a little squeeze while holding the dog's mouth at the end of the nozzle and it will soon be licking away. Keep the terrier in such a box for a few weeks and then try again. Give it a few nights and if the messing continues, then use the box again for a couple of weeks and try once more. This method has never failed when I have used it for even the most persistent of night-time 'messers'.

Lead training

Lead training is the next objective and this can be carried out in the home and around the garden, before the innoculations have been given, though never be tempted to take a puppy outside of the immediate home environment until those innoculations have taken place. Any decent pet shop will have a plentiful supply of puppy leads and collars and these are extremely cheap to purchase. Attach the collar and simply leave on for a time until the puppy is ignoring it. The collar must not be so tight that you cannot get a finger underneath, nor too loose that a pup can get a paw, or even its bottom jaw, underneath whilst trying to remove the irritating article. In no time at all, your puppy will completely ignore the collar. Now you can attach the lead and allow the youngster to become familiar with it as it drags it around, though always supervised, for a lead can easily snag and if a puppy

A Patterdale puppy.

should jump off a step, or it jumps down some other drop, it could easily hang itself.

Once the lead has been attached for a few minutes, pick it up and encourage the novice to walk with you. Inevitably, the stubborn natured terrier will pull away and refuse to co-operate. Again, this is an opportunity to establish who is in charge. Go with the puppy and you are no longer pack leader. However, by holding the lead firmly and then by dragging the youngster along, though gently, you show that you are in charge and that you will not be 'bossed'. It won't take long for the terrier to yield to your authority and very soon it will be walking with you, though probably now going to the other extreme and pulling *you* along. Again, take control of the situation and pull the puppy back to your side while commanding it firmly to 'heel'. Walking to heel is best accomplished once innoculations are completed and you can walk regularly in more open spaces. As the puppy grows, stronger collars and leads will be necessary.

Whilst carrying out lead training, you can also train a terrier for when it will appear in the ring, if you will be exhibiting of course. By pulling the lead up slightly, you can teach a puppy to stand still. While it is doing so, wave a chocolate, or a biscuit under its nose and it should stand to attention, fully alert in anticipation of receiving the treat. A terrier looks its best when standing alert and keen and having a terrier 'showing' itself in this manner can mean the difference between winning and losing.

Make training fun for both yourself and your trainee. Keep the sessions short and provide plenty of opportunities for play. After a training session, I often throw balls, the hard rubber type, which cannot be chewed up, for my youngsters and they love the chase and catching them. If one has an overgrown area in your garden (I leave a small part of my garden growing wild for the wildlife), then throw the ball into such an area and allow the puppy to search for it. This will quickly teach it to use its nose and the lesson will be applied when hunting begins later on. By putting forth that earnest effort to train a youngster, one will have a well-behaved, content pet and working dog.

A terrier will very quickly get used to travelling in cars and it is best to have them enclosed in a terrier box, or inside a steel-mesh cage where they will not make a nuisance of themselves, for a dog loose about the car can be a distraction to a driver and is in far more danger of being killed if one should have a crash. These can be on the expensive side, but will last for years and so easily pay for themselves over time. These are also very handy for keeping your terrier under control whilst attending shows, though always be aware of hot sunshine and never leave them inside cars on even warm days. Cars in hot weather, even with the windows partly open, are notorious deathtraps

Training to work.
Training a dog to hunt and work quarry is an impossibility. All one can do is to provide opportunity for work and the breeding of the dog, that is, the inbred instinct 'branded' into their personality after generations of working ancestors, will do the rest, though there are certain rules to follow.

Entering can begin on rabbits after much of the basic training

Reward and praise good behaviour.

and breaking to livestock has been accomplished at around six months of age, though this can be started sooner if one has come to trust the young entry before this time. By taking a puppy amongst rabbits, along hedgerows etc and encouraging it to chase and hunt them, one will soon have a dog that is keenly looking for its quarry and even putting its nose down. Of course, if you can work the youngster alongside an older dog, then so much the better, for they learn very quickly from their elder peers and pick up skills which may otherwise take quite some time to learn.

Patterdales make great ferreting dogs and all one has to do is take the pup along and allow it to sniff at the entrance to a warren. After netting up, enter the ferret and then dispatch the first rabbit to hit the net and allow the puppy to taste the carcass, teasing it and getting it excited. Do the same for a few trips and very soon the puppy will be hunting them, putting them up out of cover and giving chase, and, after quite a bit of experience (though some puppies mark true almost from day one), will be marking warrens as occupied, or otherwise. A marking terrier is worth its weight in gold.

If you will be working your puppy with hounds, then avoid rabbits, but otherwise there is no valid reason not to allow it to hunt them, for this activity teaches a pup the use of its nose and quickly arouses curiosity in dark tunnels – something that will be most useful when it comes to starting a terrier to its more traditional quarry: the fox.

Rats are next on the quarry list and the same principles apply, though bolting rats directly to the terrier, as opposed to nets, is the best method, for few terriers will resist the impulse to grab the fleeing rodent. This can begin at around eight months of age and few Patterdales will not erupt and kill their rat once they have been bitten, which is very often the case with a first rat, provided they are not entered too young. If a puppy does not take to killing rats on its first outing, then simply keep taking it out and I guarantee it will begin doing so before long, again, especially if it hunts alongside an adult. If one will be hunting mink, however, alongside hounds, then it is best avoiding rats, for they will hunt a rat as keenly as they will mink.

Mink are an incredibly vicious biting quarry and so a terrier is best left until it is about ten months of age before seeing such quarry. Also, mink are very difficult to catch in the first place, so one must be persistent and keep the spirits of the young entry high with regular encouragement. Take a lesson from the

Huntsman and hear how he regularly talks to his hounds while they are drawing and hunting. This keeps morale high and one can do the same with terriers. If you do get a mink to ground, do your utmost to dig it out, or bolt it, so that the terrier can claim its prize.

This is what is known as the gradual entering process and is most effective, but do not worry if one of the chain, or even all of the chain, is missed out before entering to fox, for a terrier, provided it is left until it is mentally mature, will enter straight to Reynard without any problem. Again, at around twelve months of age, give the young entry the opportunity. If a fox is marked to ground or run to ground by hounds, or maybe a lurcher, then simply allow the puppy to smell the earth and encourage it to go. If it refuses, then use another terrier, a more experienced one, and allow it to watch and listen to all of the action (before this time one should have allowed a puppy a shake of a fox carcass so that it has some idea of what life is about, but this is not always possible for the beginner, for fox carcasses are not easy to acquire). And so, if the youngster will not go, then give it a couple more months and try again.

Patience really is a virtue when it comes to working and entering terriers, for one must sometimes wait several months for a novice to catch on, though not everyone is possessed of this virtue. Brian Nuttall once sold two terrier puppies to two lads who were friends and hunting partners. One of the youngsters entered immediately to fox at around twelve months of age and rapidly made progress, while the other refused to work. At the age of thirteen months, Brian received a phone call from the frustrated chap who asked if he could swap it for another Patterdale puppy. Brian encouraged him to hang onto it and wait until it was at least eighteen months of age before giving up on it, but he would not listen and so Nuttall complied with his wishes and swapped it for another.

This bitch, Sophie, now at the age of sixteen months, was taken to a meet of the Cotswold foxhounds and a fox was run to ground in a twelve-inch drainpipe. Brian was going to put her in behind another, more experienced terrier, but she seemed keen to go on her own and so, risking a great deal of embarrassment should she refuse, loosed her alone. She shot into the pipe, scrambled up it, bolted a fox and then promptly found a second, which she then finished below ground in double-quick time. The bitch, as they say, never looked back after this and had that lad waited just a few more months he would have had a superb worker on his hands.

Brian also tells a tale of Racket, another Patterdale bitch of his breeding, which would not enter at the age of sixteen months. He was with a keeper who shot a fox at the time. The bitch was allowed to go to the fresh carcass, but she would not touch it and Brian was mocked by the keeper who said that the bitch would never work.

At the age of twenty-two months Nuttall took this still un-entered bitch down to the same keepered estate and she suddenly caught on. Nuttall enjoyed an easy dig with her to begin with, digging down to his fox which was keenly worked by the bitch in just half an hour. The next dig saw her keen to go and they had a second fox dug out in just one hour. Again, Racket was keen to go and this time the dig lasted six and a half hours, with another fox finally being secured. The keeper remarked on what a superb terrier she was, but couldn't believe it when Nuttall proudly informed him that this was the same bitch which had refused to even look at a dead fox during his previous visit!

The lesson is to be patient and give a dog a chance. Provide it with the opportunity and, eventually, once maturity is reached, the young entry will go. Finding and staying ability cannot be taught to a puppy, for this must be in the breeding, though, as I have already stated, a youngster will learn much by watching an experienced terrier at work.

These same principles apply in whatever country one hunts and whatever quarry one seeks. The American badger is one of the fiercest quarry a Patterdale will face and mental maturity is essential when up to such prey. A terrier will go when it is ready, but I would advise waiting until at least twelve months of age before giving a youngster its first opportunity of working larger quarry. And, learn a lesson from Frank Buck and other noted terriermen: always try to dispatch your quarry as quickly and as humanely as possible.

11

BREEDING

Both the stud dog and brood bitch must be good-natured with people, especially children, and other dogs, and must have proven themselves both biddable and good workers, if work is what is required of the offspring, and most Patterdale owners do work their charges, though a growing number of these terriers are enjoying life as family pets.

A breeder with a good reputation will have excellent stud dogs standing for the service of suitable bitches and one can expect to pay anything from £50 upwards of the price of a puppy at around £200. Asking the price of a pup is not unreasonable as the other stud fee, and one requested by some owners of stud dogs, is to have pick of the litter.

A black and chocolate pup out of the same litter (Dilly x Gomez).

It is a good idea to make contact with the owner of a suitable stud dog and, if he or she lives within easy reach, then ask to see the dog beforehand, making certain that it is well-behaved and socialised. A terrier keen to latch onto anything that crosses its path and completely ignores its 'master's' commands must be avoided like the plague.

Preparations must be made *before* the bitch has even come into season. First of all, take note of the previous season and mark on the calendar when the next one, the one when she will be mated, is due to occur. This can easily be done, for the first heat should not be the one when she is put to the chosen stud dog, and this first season may occur at six months, or even as late as twelve months. Even then, if you are going to be breeding from a proven worker, you must wait until the bitch has served for at least one season. This is a good guide to follow, for a bitch will not usually be mentally mature at even twelve months, so it is best to wait until her third or fourth heat, depending on whether a bitch begins her heats at six, or twelve months of age. A month or so before she is due, give the bitch a multi-wormer and rid her of any fleas, for it is these annoying little parasites which will re-infest a bitch and her pups with worms (these remedies can be purchased at any veterinary surgery, or pet shop). This diligence will make certain that she is worm-free when conception takes place, meaning that she will be in the best condition possible.

Another task to have completed before your bitch has come in season is to have a whelping box at hand. This can be made of wood, or you may find that a very sturdy cardboard box, of the type used for packing electrical goods, is suitable. There must be plenty of room for the bitch to spread out and her litter to play as they grow and the sides must be deep enough to keep draughts off the litter and the puppies inside, for one does not want a riot of puppies all over the house, chewing and messing as they go. Also, the dam must be able to get in and out of the box easily enough without the pups following. The sides must be high enough to accomplish this restriction of the litter, yet low enough to allow the bitch to see her pups, so that she does not jump in and land on one of them, possibly injuring one or more of her youngsters.

Having all of this done, all one has to do now is to alert the owner of the stud dog of the approximate date the season is due and wait for it to happen. The vulva will begin swelling and bleeding will begin shortly afterwards, so be diligent and check her every day, for you must count the days from when bleeding begins. Fertility begins at around nine or ten days after the bleeding starts and I advise that the twelfth day is the best time to have her mated. If you are travelling quite some distance and if there is a spare kennel, the owner of the stud dog may allow you to leave your bitch with him for a couple of days, during which time he will allow mating to occur again, usually on the fourteenth day.

The bitch should be held, but if she will not stand, simply allow the pair to run loose together, for she may not stand until quite a bit of play and fuss has occurred. Even then, she may keep snapping at the dog and warning him off. If so, try again the next day, or in a couple of days time. Once she is standing, hold her still and allow the dog to work alone, unless he is having obvious difficulties. An experienced handler of a stud dog will then help 'guide' the dog until penetration is successful. The pair will then become tied together and this must happen if conception is going to occur. Once tied, help the dog to get his leg over (no pun intended) the back end of the bitch so that they are back to back with each other and then hold them there until separation occurs. This can take only a few minutes, or, more often than not, anything up to an hour or so, though I would say that twenty minutes to half an hour is about the average time it takes for a dog and bitch to separate. Whilst tied, the dog will continue to pump sperm into the bitch and this almost guarantees a successful coupling.

Pregnancy
For the first four or five weeks of pregnancy, life can carry on as normal for a bitch and exercise and work need not be restricted. During that fifth week of pregnancy, one extra meal a day should be provided and I give this first thing in the morning. I normally give a Weetabix, or something similar, with plenty of milk (watered-down a little to avoid scouring) and, as the weeks pass, increase the quantity. A drink of milk with a touch of glucose added after her evening meal is also appropriate at this time, but warm it and take the chill out and, again, water it down a little, for milk is rich and can easily upset her stomach.

At seven weeks into pregnancy, if you feel it is necessary, a third meal can be added, at lunchtime. This can be a slice of wholemeal bread with slightly warmed, watered-down milk. She will be showing signs of pregnancy by the fifth week, but will be bulging all over the place by the seventh. From the fifth week onward, work must stop and exercise be curtailed, lessening with each passing week until she can only manage a very short walk in the late stages of pregnancy. Do not stop exercise at all though, right up until whelping begins, for she must be kept fit if she is going to cope well with the birth. Of course, the bitch must be fit and well exercised before mating occurs, but it is important to maintain that fitness during pregnancy.

The seventh week is now the time to prepare the whelping box for the soon-to-be nursing mother. If you use a cardboard box, and I recommend that you do if you can find one sturdy enough, then a good tip is to cut out a door in one of the walls of the box, just wide enough to allow the bitch through, but just cut down the two sides and leave it as a flap. While the pups are young, one can simply leave the opening very low, allowing easier access for the bitch as she comes and goes. As the pups grow and become more mobile, one can raise the height of the door in order to prevent their escape. It is a practical system which works very well indeed.

There is no need to provide multi-vitamins, or any other kind of supplements, during either pregnancy, or the nursing stages, but a well-balanced diet is essential: one that provides the necessary amounts of fat, proteins and calcium. Milk will provide calcium, but another good tip is to dry eggshells in the oven and then crush them into a fine powder. Sprinkle this on the evening meal which should be meat and biscuits, and a superb source of calcium will be provided. Also, give her the egg in a little milk, or even boil, or poach the egg first, if you are worried about giving raw eggs, for this is a rich source of vitamins. By providing enough meat, biscuits, cereals and milk, however, one will ensure that the bitch, and thus the puppies, will remain healthy and active.

A generous layer of newspaper can be placed in the whelping box as this material is easily disposed of and replaced, so weeks before the birth is due, collect a substantial pile of old newspapers, saving those you buy and asking friends and family for theirs. Believe me, you are going to need quite a lot of this bedding material, especially once the puppies are mobile and messing quite frequently.

Labour
Settle the bitch in the whelping box during the seventh week and then await the beginning of labour. Once that full nine week term

has concluded (though they can be either a little early, or a little late), she will become ever more uncomfortable and restless. She will begin making her bed as pains afflict her, but keep a close eye on her and do not allow her to get into dark, dingy corners from where you cannot reach her, for she may attempt to give birth outside in a chosen spot. She will lose her appetite as the time to give birth approaches and she may vomit, often becoming panicky, especially if this is her first litter. Do not worry, for this is completely normal behaviour and your steady hand and nerves of steel will help her along, for if you panic, you will only make her even more unsettled, so do your best to comfort her. This behaviour could also continue for quite some time, hours in fact, so do not hope for a quick end to the situation.

Always make sure she has plenty of water available at this time, for, though she will probably refuse food, she may wish to drink quite a bit. Labour is now well along, once you notice her straining and pushing. She will have lost a steady flow of discharge throughout her pregnancy, but much more fluid will come away now. This is the time for extra vigilance on your part. Problems are quite rare, especially in terrier breeds, so there is little to worry about, but still, keep a close eye on things. Often, a litter already birthed, done and dusted, will greet you in the morning, but if the bitch is a first time mum, then she may make such a fuss that she will wake the whole household. If outside in a kennel, then be even more diligent before going to bed, for, if there are signs that labour has begun, it is best to sit up with your bitch in order to make certain there are no complications.

Especially during autumn, winter and spring, use heat lamps in a kennel in order to keep the nightly chill from off the whelps, for at least the first three weeks. Even in summer, heat lamps will help a litter get through their first few nights of life, unless the weather is unusually warm.

It will not take too long for the first pup to appear at the vulva, but if your bitch strains for quite some time without result and her strength and interest is fast waning, then get onto your vet and ask for immediate assistance. It may be a good idea to inform your vet of the date the pups are due, so that he can be prepared for a possible emergency. Do not go poking around inside the bitch yourself, but leave it to the professionals. If a pup appears and seems stuck, however, then, after thoroughly washing your hands, help it on its way by pulling very gently at the same time as the bitch is pushing.

Some pups will come out head first, while others will come out rear end first, but do not worry about this, for it is quite normal. Once clear of the vagina, the bitch will lick off the protective sack and this will start the pups breathing. Also, she will bite the cord a little way from the body, thus separating the pup from the afterbirth, which the bitch will eat. Do not try to prevent her, for this is nature's way of keeping the nest clean and of providing the bitch with essential nutrients that will help her to regain strength and pass on goodness to her pups.

Problems are not uncommon at this stage, but do not worry, for they are easily dealt with. Have a pair of blunt scissors and a roughish old towel, or flannel, handy. If the dam fails to remove the sack, then gently rub the pup with the flannel dampened with warm water and this will act in much the same manner as the dam's tongue. The wriggling pup may now stir the bitch into action, but if not, then use the blunt scissors to cut the cord well away from the body. Hernias can occur when the cord is not bitten soon after birth, so be quick about doing this if the bitch fails to do her duty.

An afterbirth should follow each pup into the outside world, but this is not always the case, for two pups, twins if you like, can share the same afterbirth. In this case, a pup will be born and, if the bitch fails to bite the cord, will be fully out of the vagina, but will be hanging from the cord, thus making the risk of a hernia, or even of being crushed by the dam sitting on it, even more likely, so get in there and cut the cord so that the puppy is free. The afterbirth will not come until the other twin has been born. Count the afterbirths and, if in doubt, get your vet to examine her, for retained afterbirths can make a bitch very ill, even kill her if not dealt with quickly enough.

Labour can last for several hours and, once all of the pups have been born, your bitch will be incredibly deflated. Once birthing is over, your bitch will obviously cease pushing and straining and will instead concentrate on her new litter. This is now the time to allow your bitch to go outside in order to empty herself whilst you very quickly clean out the whelping box, replacing the old soiled newspaper with new. The dam will have already taken a lot of persuading to leave her brood, so be quick about it, for she will soon be back. Once safely back in the nest, offer her a drink of slightly warmed milk, but do not give her food just yet, for she will have eaten the afterbirths. This may make her scour for a day or so, but do not worry, for this will soon cease.

Care of the new-born puppies

Now is not the time to relax however, for you will still need to keep a close eye on things, though do not be worrying, for problems are rare. Milk fever can strike during those first few days in particular, but is rare and easily treated with a calcium injection. The symptoms to watch out for are restlessness, rapid breathing and lapsing into convulsions or fits of excessive trembling. Call the vet in immediately should this, or any other serious matter, occur.

The dam will be very protective of her family, so keep other pets and children well away from the litter for the first few days in particular, though she must be watched even after this. If one keeps ferrets, or any other type of predator, as a pet, or even as a working animal, and you normally allow them to be loose around the house, then refrain from doing so at this time, for a ferret will easily kill young puppies, even up to the age of three months or

Dilly and her son Piper. Dilly is out of Nick Stevens' Patterdales. Piper was sired by Dave Finlay's Gomez.

so. Ferrets should be caged well away from puppies and measures taken to ensure that a fitch cannot escape and reach them.

There is now little to do, but to watch the litter grow and make certain that the whelping box is kept clean and the bitch well fed and watered. She will not usually leave the puppies for the first few days, so exercise will not take place, just short breaks into the garden, but, once she will leave her litter for a while, then begin exercising her again, though for only short walks at first. Work must not begin again until the pups are at least five or six weeks of age, when they are fully weaned and much less dependant on their dam. Even then, much has been taken out of her and I would give her a rest period before starting to take her out hunting again.

Stroke and handle the puppies, though very gently, as soon as the dam will allow this, for this is going to help immensely, the socialising process. As they grow, handle them more and more and play with them often. Also, teach your children how to handle them and play with them properly, not allowing them to be carried about the place which could result in a dropped, and thus dead, puppy, but certainly allowing them to nurse puppies on their lap. This will ensure that the litter will grow to be suitable as both working dogs, intelligent and easily trained, and family pets, for Patterdales can quite easily cope with both roles at the same time.

In Britain, according to law, one must have a puppy's tail docked by a qualified veterinary surgeon. I must say that this is far better than doing the job yourself. I have docked quite a few litters of terrier puppies when it was legal to do so and there is far more bleeding than when this is carried out by the vet. True, a blunt pair of scissors will be used and the pain will be the same, no matter who carries out the procedure, but a vet will use a silver-nitrate stick, which acts as a rapid blood-clotting agent that stops the bleeding immediately. The cost is low too, at only £5 a pup (at time of writing), so it is well worth having the job done professionally, even if you are not required to do so by the law of your country.

However, if you are intent on doing the job yourself (and it is legal in your country), then it must be done properly. The procedure is best carried out at three days and no earlier, though it can be done up to the fifth day. You will need a pair of small, blunt scissors, a silver nitrate stick if one can get hold of such a thing (there are stores which sell veterinary supplies to the public in some countries) and some antibiotic powder, though medicated talc will suffice if one cannot get hold of this.

Having a helpful companion is also essential as they need to hold the puppy still while the procedure is carried out. Leave just over half of the tail on and simply snip the rest off with the scissors. If you can obtain proper docking scissors from a retailers, all the better, but a normal pair will do the job just as effectively. The puppy will squeal a little and the cut will inevitably bleed. Apply the nitrate stick to the end of it, or dip the wound into medicated talc, or, preferably, antibiotic powder which will help thicken and thus clot the blood – stopping the bleeding fairly quickly. The dam must be well out of the way whilst the operation is undertaken, for hearing her puppies squeal will cause her much distress.

The puppies feel a little pain, but docking is certainly not cruel. I have seen them go straight back to sleep again immediately after the procedure has been carried out and they show no adverse effects whatsoever. When a silver-nitrate stick is not used, then the bleeding will continue for some time. The bitch may lick at the tails and this can start the bleeding again, so continue to dip them in talc, or antibiotic powder, changing the newspaper for fresh whenever it becomes soiled with the blood. As I have stated, I feel that a veterinary surgeon is the best option, but I am a realist and know that many will carry out the procedure themselves, so always be hygienic when doing so, sterilising instruments by boiling them up in water before use and thoroughly cleansing your hands. If you can obtain them, wear surgical gloves whilst carrying out tail docking.

Worming the bitch and puppies should be carried out when they are two weeks of age, or whenever the remedy used advises. I use the chocolate flavoured liquid for treating roundworms (puppies and nursing bitches must not be treated for tapeworms) and this is most effective. The dose is according to weight and so it is advisable to weigh the pups before dosing them. Kitchen scales are ideal for this. A fully-grown Patterdale terrier bitch will weigh anything from 10lb to 17lb (4.5kg to 7.7kg) and so you must dose accordingly. Always follow the instructions, which may tell you to dose every two weeks until the puppies reach eight weeks, the age at which they will be sold off to their new homes.

It can be quite an awkward job dosing unweaned puppies, so I use a plastic syringe (without the needle of course) and slowly

Weaning black and chocolate Patterdale pups at 4 weeks. Bred out of Dilly
(Nick Stevens) and JC (Dave Finlay).

pump the liquid into their mouth. As they grow, one can put this
onto their food, if you are willing to feed them one at a time, but
I find it best to continue using the syringe method.

The eyes will begin to open at around the age of two weeks,
though some may be later than others. They do not see clearly at
first, but the grey mist will soon begin to fade and the eyes will
soon clearly be seen. At three weeks of age, the puppies will begin
walking around the bed, though very unsteadily at first, until the
strength begins to build in the bones and muscles. They will be
quite mobile by the fourth week and from then on progress is
rapid. I do not wean until four weeks of age. True, if the mother's
milk begins to dry up before this time, then it is safe to wean
sooner, but is unnecessary when the bitch has plenty to offer. I
use Weetabix, a type of wheat cereal biscuit, or something similar,
softened with slightly warmed, watered-down milk, for weaning,
as this is easily lapped up, swallowed and digested. Feed this
meal twice a day for the first few days when it will be safe to add
another meal consisting of meat. Tinned puppy food is ideal and

full of the goodness needed for a growing litter. Give them the meat alone and do not add specially prepared puppy biscuits until they reach six weeks of age, when they will better cope with them. If, at this age, they seem satisfied with two meals, then continue thus until it is obvious they need another. If, on increasing to three meals, they seem unsatisfied, then by all means add another meal, two of cereal and milk, and two of meat and biscuits.

The whelping box will need to be cleaned several times a day after the third week. The bitch will have kept the nest clean up until that time, but it is a kindness, and a necessity for the sake of hygiene, to help out in the cleaning department and give her less to do. The bitch should enjoy light exercise for the first four weeks, but be careful not to let her off the lead, for she may abandon you and head back to her youngsters. This can place her in great danger of either being picked up by someone who thinks she is lost, stolen, or even worse, knocked down by a car. From the fourth week, exercise can be increased until she is back in her normal routine. Continue with the extra feeding, but if she is putting weight on, then cut out one of the meals, or reduce quantity, or, on the other hand, if she is losing weight, then increase quantity. Set rules are useless in these cases, for each individual dog is different, so one must be vigilant and respond to her needs, and the needs of her family, accordingly.

The puppies, right up until it is time to sell them on to good homes, are best kept confined in their whelping box, but, two or three times a day, it is a good idea to allow them out to exercise: in your garden if it is escape-proof and other animals which may spread infectious diseases cannot get in, or around the home. At these times, always be aware of safety issues and make certain there are no wires that can be chewed, or heavy objects which can fall on and crush a puppy. Also, do not leave buckets of water around where a pup is in danger of falling in and drowning. A drink of watered-down milk should be given to puppies after every meal, but otherwise they will get fluids from the bitch, so there is no need to leave large bowls of water around for them, though the dam must always have access to fresh water.

Always supervise children too, for they must be taught to handle and play with puppies very gently, for a badly treated pup will have its socialising adversely affected. A well-treated puppy will grow into a friendly, trustworthy adult, so keep a close eye on chldren and make sure they know how to handle them properly.

If you will be keeping one of the puppies, then make your choice and keep this one out of the way when viewers arrive, for someone is sure to want the one you have chosen and they may go away disappointed. To attract buyers, one must advertise the litter in local newspapers, or in a dog magazine which has a wide readership.

You will undoubtedly do your best to make certain that the puppies go to good homes, but, nevertheless, you will be saddened by their departure. After eight weeks of helping to rear and look after them, however, it will no doubt bring relief to have a little peace in your life once more, though the house will feel empty, after those bundles of energy and mischief have gone!

12

COMMON AILMENTS
AND INJURIES

These are just a few problems that the Patterdale owner may encounter. When in any doubt consult your veterinary surgeon.

Bites
Different quarry species will inflict different kinds of bites and in different areas, but all can be treated in the same way. First of all, thoroughly clean the area to be treated with clean water. Once all the muck is washed away, using cotton wool, or make-up remover pads which are ideal for the task, thoroughly wash out the bites with generously salted water, but make sure that you keep this well away from the eyes. Wounds close to the eyes should be treated with clean water alone and nothing else. Also, for deeper bites, the nib of a syringe, without the needle, can be placed into the wound and salt water flushed into it. This will wash out any pieces of muck lodged therein and will help the healing process greatly. After cleaning is finished, apply iodine to the bites with a piece of cotton wool. For the first few days, wash the bites three or four times a day, but leave untreated with creams as the fresh air must get to the wounds and dry them up. Generally, bites will heal without antibiotics, but more serious bites must be treated with these, or with a penicillin injection. This applies to bites from larger quarry only, for rat and mink bites, if thoroughly cleaned, will usually heal very quickly and without causing undue problems.

Constipation
A dose of liquid paraffin is a tried and tested method of relieving constipation which will manifest itself in a lack of droppings and a dog straining to go to the toilet without result. Again, persistent constipation is best treated by your local vet.

Cuts

Minor cuts can simply be cleaned with iodine, or a good, strong antiseptic lotion. Major cuts will need stitching by a qualified veterinary surgeon. After watching a vet at work, many take up stitching themselves. If you will be doing your own stitching, then make certain that the needle and thread are sterilised and wear sterilised surgical gloves to carry out the procedure. Stitching a wound may also be backed-up by a course of anti-biotics, but in some countries such as Southern Ireland, penicillin can be bought over the counter at chemist shops. An injection according to the instructions on the bottle will do much to guard against infection, though sprinkling the wound with anti-biotic powder will also help.

Ear canker and mites

Excessive scratching of the ears will signal that something is amiss. Usually canker, or ear mites, are to blame and treatments obtained over the counter at pet stores will usually be suitable for treating both of these complaints at the same time. When used maybe once a year, these ear-drops can be preventitive of such complaints appearing in the first place. Simply follow the instructions, but if symptoms persist, again, veterinary treatment will be necessary. If you keep more than one dog, then all will need treating, for ear mites easily spread between dogs. With both eye and ear complaints, it is essential never to go poking around and trying to sort out the problem oneself, for much damage could be done to these delicate organs. After trying basic treatments, always allow the professionals to deal with more persistent problems.

Mange

Excessive scratching, bald patches, and irritated skin, are the symptoms to watch for and this can be a most serious condition. Early treatment is very effective, however, so do not delay in getting your dog checked out by a vet. The problem may simply be some kind of allergy, such as doggy hay fever, which manifests itself in skin complaints. The vet will usually administer a steroid injection to deal with the problem, which may, alas, recur in the future.

Scouring (diarrhoea)

Dogs are terrible scroungers, known as carrion eaters in the wild, and will pick up and eat almost anything edible, despite the fact that it was unfit for consumption a long time past, and so scouring can be a fairly common complaint. The most effective cure for this is simply to starve your terrier for twenty-four hours, making sure that clean, fresh water is available at all times. Restrict exercise too, as this will prevent them from picking up any more bits of stale food, which will only prolong the problem. If the symptoms persist, then try a little arrowroot mixed in warm milk, given a few times throughout the day.

If the symptoms still persist, or the scouring is accompanied by vomiting, not being able to keep anything, even water, down, then consult your vet, for the problem is likely to be gastroenteritis and this is serious and must be treated immediately. Also, if the scouring is accompanied by excessive drinking of water, another symptom of gastro-entiritis, then the problem needs to be addressed by a vet as soon as possible.

Snake bites
The type of snake that bites a dog will differ depending on the country one inhabits. The important thing is to know your snakes and quickly identify the culprit so that the correct treatment can be given. After speaking with your vet, ask if it is possible, if you hunt rural areas where getting to a vet in a short time is impossible, for you to carry the antidote to the most common venom of the snakes in that area. Otherwise, get your dog to a vet immediately for treatment, as most poisonous snake bites, even with adders in Britain, are fatal to an untreated dog.

Stings
Bee stings are the worst, for they will leave the sting in the skin. Remove this carefully with tweezers and wash with an antiseptic wipe, or spray with an antiseptic spray. Wasp stings can be treated in the same way, but one must keep a close eye on the dog for a period of time afterwards, for, like humans, some animals are adversely affected by stings and they must be treated by a vet immediately.

Watery eyes
Often called a 'cold in the eye', this problem is easily treated. Simply boil some water and allow it to cool until lukewarm. Using cotton wool, clean the eye three or four times a day. If symptoms persist after a couple of days, then get your dog checked out by a vet. More serious eye and ear complaints must

be treated by a vet. Watery eyes can also be caused by muck getting into them, especially after a session below ground, or whilst ratting, and these can be treated in the same way, though effective eye washes can be obtained from your local pet store.

The first-aid kit
This should consist of cotton wool, a syringe, a pair of tweezers, a bottle of clean water and a bottle of generously salted water, antiseptic wipes, or spray, or, preferably, iodine, a bottle of penicillin and a sterilised needle and syringe. A stitching needle and suture material, if one is brave enough to do your own stitching (only after having seen a vet do the job), can also be included. This can be kept in your car, or even in your bag, so that first-aid can be carried out immediately.

Appendices

1
Bibliography

For more information on Patterdales and their work see:

The Traditional Working Terrier, Sean Frain, Swan Hill Press, 2001.

The Fell Terrier, D. Brian Plummer, The Boydell Press, 1983.

The Sporting Terrier, D. Brian Plummer, The Boydell Press, 1992.

The World of the Working Terrier, David Harcombe, Fieldfare Publications, 1989.

The Modern Working Terrier, Michael Shaw, The Boydell Press, 1985.

2
Useful Addresses

The Countryman's Weekly, Yelverton, Devon, PL20 7PE

Earth Dog, Running Dog, Fieldfare, P.O. Box 2, Llandeilo, Dyfed, SA19 6EW

3
The Breeding of Some of Nuttall's Patterdale Terriers

Turk (born March 1952). Parents: Bracken and Nip. Grandparents: (Bracken) Copper and Brandy. (Nip) Tanner and Tansy.

Flint (1) (sold to Kevin Powers and born in May 1969). Parents: Ben and Whip. Grandparents: (Ben) Turk and Bugg. (Whip) Kipper (Wally Wild) and Tar.

Barney (born in August 1983 and sold to Steve Harcombe). Parents: Jet and Nipper. Grandparents: (Jet) Blitz and Blacky. (Nipper) Blitz (2) and Key.

Miner (born in July 1989). Parents: Cagney and Nessie. Grandparents: (Cagney) Borderer and Fire. (Nessie) Jetson and Thatcher.

Blackie (born in September 1991 and later sold to Gordon Mason). Parents: Rastus and Lucky. Grandparents: (Rastus) Tallant and Tugger. (Lucky) Miner and Saddler.

INDEX

advertise 205
afterbirth 199
Akerigg, Josie 67, 71, 72, 80, 119, 121, 163
Apprentice 101

bedding 197
Bingo (Bing) viii, ix, 70, 72, 73, 81, 86, 98, 163
bites 206
Bobbery Packs 47
Bowman, Joe 17, 40, 41
brawn 179
Breay, Cyril viii, 11, 29, 53, 57, 59, 61–74, 76–83, 85, 91–3, 96–101, 105, 110–14, 118–22, 125, 127, 128, 132, 135, 136, 139, 140, 143–5, 147, 152, 153, 155, 157, 162, 163
breeding 194–205
of Nuttall's terriers 211
Buck, Frank viii, 10–12, 19, 20, 29, 59, 61, 64, 65, 67–74, 76–83, 85–7, 91–3, 96–101, 105, 110–16, 118–22, 127, 128, 132, 135, 136, 138–45, 147–55, 157, 158, 162, 163, 147
Buck, Max 68, 138–40, 142–53, 155, 163, 174
Bulldogs 31

cockerel 11
'Chowt-Faced' Rock 38, 39, 44, 47, 48

constipation 206
convulsions 200
Coquetdale terrier 29
Corgi 95
Corby 40, 43, 44
cutting the cord 199
cow-hide bones 181
cuts 207

Davey, Black 98, 101, 120, 135
Daz 143, 144, 152, 153
Decies, Lord 41, 44
diarrhoea 207
distemper 179
Dove Crag 12

ear canker 207
entering 101, 102, 134, 151, 190–3

first aid 206–9
first aid kit 209
fox drives 7
foxwarren 49

gunpacks 9
Gould, Ken 55, 56, 58, 83, 112, 116, 118, 157, 174
Heelway 33, 34
house training 186–8

innoculations 179
Irving, Willie 26

Kelly 24

212

kennelling 180, 181
Kipper 72, 73, 86, 98

Lasty 72, 121, 122, 163
lead training 188–90
leptosprosis 134, 179
lie-down 185
Lill Foiler 25, 40, 58
livestock breaking 166, 182
Lowther Castle strain 15, 29, 46

mange 207
mating 196
milk fever 200
mineshafts 20, 21
mites 207

nitrate, silver 201, 202
Nuttall, Brian 71, 80, 82, 83, 85, 91, 96–101, 103–5, 108–10, 113, 118–20, 122, 125–7, 129, 135, 138–40, 153, 164, 171, 174, 175, 192, 193

Parson Russell 25, 58
Parvo-virus 179
pets 163–70, 174
Porter of Borrowdale 4
pregnancy 196–7
puppies, care and training 177–93, 200, 205

rabies 179
Redesdale terrier 29
Reedwater terrier 29
Rif, Bradley's 31, 32, 64, 65

Rothbury terrier 29,
Rusty 72, 73, 98

sit 185
skiffle 53, 153
shoots 8, 9, 111
showing 153–62
Smithy 83, 110, 118
snake bites 208
stay 185, 186
stings 208
stud 28, 53, 56, 58, 66, 83, 88, 99, 158, 194, 195, 196

tail docking 201, 202
Tess 111, 112, 114
Tex 138, 143, 150, 163
Tip 25, 58

Vic 11, 25

watery eyes 208
weaning 203
websites for Patterdales 175
whelping 197–9
whelping box 195, 197, 201, 204
Westmoreland, Roger ix, 22, 23, 28, 29, 47, 59, 62, 67, 68, 69, 71–3, 78, 80, 98, 141, 143
worming and treating fleas 181, 182, 195, 202
Wilkinson's Rock 52, 53, 55, 56, 70, 101, 116

Zetland 121, 163